Covent Garden Market

Its History and Restoration

Covent Garden Market

Its History and Restoration

Robert Thorne

Historic Buildings Division
Greater London Council
Department of Architecture
and Civic Design

The Architectural Press: London

First published in 1980 by
The Architectural Press Ltd: London

ISBN 0 85139 098 6 (cloth)
ISBN 0 85139 099 4 (paper)

Graphics and Book Design
John Beake

Editorial Control
John Earl
David Atwell

Frontispiece:
*The west front of the market, a
photograph taken after the two iron
roofs had been added to the building.*

Printed and bound in Great Britain
by W & J Mackay Limited, Chatham.

Contents

Acknowledgements

In writing this book I have depended heavily on the support and advice of my colleagues in the GLC Historic Buildings Division and the Covent Garden Team who have been willing to put aside time during the most hectic period of the restoration to discuss the project with me. On the history of the market and its buildings I owe an equal debt to Mrs Marie P G Draper, Archivist to the Trustees of the Bedford Estates, for her kindness in looking out the relevant records and clarifying some of the more obscure points in them. I have also received valuable help from Dr P J Atkins, Mr Kenneth Monro, Mr A G Overton of T J Poupart Ltd, Ms G M Richardson, Mr Ray Stenning of Donaldsons, Mr P D Stephens Director of the London Transport Museum, Mr A O Thorold, Mr David Webb of the Bishopsgate Institute, and Mr Ronald Webber.

My study of the Faneuil Hall Marketplace in Boston Massachusetts was greatly helped by discussions with a number of people who were involved with it in one way or another, especially Mr Roger Lang, Mr William L Mc Queen, Mr C P Monkhouse, Mr Benjamin and Mrs Jane Thompson, and Mr Roger Webb.

R T

Acknowledgements for illustrations

Jack Adams 40. Hugh Aylett 60. Peter Baistow 75. Batsford Ltd 22, 32. Timothy Bidwell 47. Birmingham Public Libraries Local Studies Department 17. Roy Bowles 4. British Museum Department of Prints and Drawings 3, 5, 66. John Clenshaw 53. The Covent Garden Market Authority 15, 28, 33. Frank Evans 35. Exeter City Council (The Royal Albert Memorial Museum) 18. Alan Fagan 1. Daryl Fowler 53. Garnett, Cloughley Blackmore and Associates 58. GLC Photographic Collection 29, 43, 44, 46, 48, 49, 50, 51, 54, 57, 65, 67. GLC Print Collection 71. GLC Survey of London draftsmen 37, 38, 39, 42 (39 and 42 revised by Robert Weston). John Michael Design Consultants 59. The Kodak Museum 14, 26, 30. The London Fire Brigade 70. London Transport Museum 61, 62. Ian McCaig 52, 53. Linda A McCauley 64. G H Marwood Esq 2. The Marquess of Tavistock and the Trustees of the Bedford Estates 6, 7, 8, 10, 11, 12, 13, 20, 21, 24, 69. Kenneth Monro Esq 72. The Museum of London 23. The National Monuments Record 27. Photo-Reportage Ltd 76. Radio Times Hulton Picture Library Frontispiece. Royal Institute of British Architects 9, 19. Royal Photographic Society 31. Bill Weims 63. Westminster City Libraries 16, 68.

Figures 1 and 72 are based on the Ordnance Survey Map with permission of the Controller of Her Majesty's Stationery Office, Crown Copyright reserved.

Foreword

Cherries so red, strawberries ripe
At home, of course, they'll be storming.
Never mind the abuse,
You have the excuse,
You went to Covent Garden in the morning.

The words of this famous old music hall song sadly perhaps no longer apply. Never again will the Royal Opera House audience emerging into the night breathe those pungent and evocative market smells – vegetables, fruit and flowers; nor will they have to push their way past lorries and stacks of crates. The Covent Garden of *My Fair Lady* has gone forever now that the market has moved to Nine Elms.

Following the departure of the market there have been many uncertainties about changes in the area. There can however be no doubt that the restoration and reuse of the central market building will have a vital influence on its future character.

The story of the central market building is a fascinating one. Covent Garden is one of London's most important and best preserved historic neighbourhoods. It can also be said to be the birthplace of modern town planning in London. The Piazza, as conceived by Inigo Jones in 1630–1, was certainly an innovatory venture, not only in terms of town planning and architectural design but also as a pioneering estate development.

Charles Fowler's new market building of 1828–30, like its less permanent predecessors, was an intrusion on Jones's Piazza layout, but it can now be recognised as a work of major importance in its own right. It was designed as a fine classical building of formal dignity, yet flexible enough to embrace the complex demands of a wholesale and retail market. Now that the market has left, it has proved itself to be readily adaptable to the needs of our own time.

Discussions about the preservation and reuse of the building started almost as soon as the decision was taken in 1964 that the business of the market was to be relocated elsewhere. The Greater London Council purchased it with other properties in 1974 and was able to start work on the first phase of the restoration within weeks of the market use coming to an end. The complex task of restoring and adapting it to new uses, the results of which can now be seen, has taken six years.

The building's architectural qualities, overlaid and obscured for more than a lifetime by additions and temporary structures, have now been revealed with such dramatic effect that it is almost as if London had gained a completely new architectural ornament. The gain is, however, more than a visual one. The Fowler market is no dead monument. It is to be used and enjoyed, to become again a lively, bustling place filled with diverse activity and paying its way commercially. This historic centre of Covent Garden has become London's newest attraction.

The restoration of the market is itself an event of significance and one which should be properly recorded. The achievement is worthy of celebration but our purpose in publishing this book is not mere self-congratulation. Robert Thorne has produced a rounded history of the market from its foundation in the seventeenth century to the reopening of the Fowler building in 1980. He has looked at all the issues – many of them quite contentious and still the subject of lively debate – which have arisen over the restoration. By relating the whole story in a frank and factual way, bringing the keen eye of the historian to recent events as well as those of the more distant past, he makes it possible for us to measure precisely what has been achieved at Covent Garden.

In the preparation of this account the author has been greatly helped (as were Dr Sheppard and his colleagues in preparing the *Survey of London* volume on the parish of St Paul's Covent Garden) by the Trustees of the Bedford Estates in granting access to the estate archives. Information and advice about the restoration have been given freely by everyone involved.

It is worth mentioning that, in all the arguments that have raged over the Covent Garden area, political bias has hardly ever influenced decisions about the Fowler building. I am proud to have been associated for the last ten years with this, the biggest single project ever entrusted to the Historic Buildings Committee and the largest restoration contract ever undertaken by the Historic Buildings Division. It has attracted world-wide attention and the resulting demand for a detailed account has now been worthily met.

I warmly commend this book to all interested in the history of London and town planning. It demonstrates how an important historic building can be sympathetically restored and happily transformed to serve a new purpose.

William Bell
Chairman, GLC Historic Buildings Committee

Chapter 1
The Making of the Market

Markets of any kind have a habit of spilling out from the building which houses them or the area to which they are supposedly confined. Market vehicles jam the approaches to them and parasite activities fill the surrounding streets. Until the market moved out in 1974 this was as true of Covent Garden as anywhere. Although the market was not planned as part of the development of the district, once successfully established it followed the familiar course of infecting everything around it. The confusion that lay in the area and the market having the same name was symbolised, for the layman at least, by the difficulty of distinguishing where each began and ended. On the same count it is impossible to discuss the market and its buildings without considering the pattern of landownership and development in the area that it came to dominate.

Historically the proper boundaries of the area are those of the parish of St Paul's Covent Garden but their shape cannot be understood without reference to the boundaries of the Bedford Estate, the land granted by the Crown to John Russell, 1st Earl of Bedford in 1541 and 1552 (Figure 1). The transfer of this land, which had belonged to the Abbey or Convent of St Peter at Westminster, was part of the widespread break-up of religious estates following the Reformation in which loyal court servants such as Russell were liberally rewarded. The two grants covered an area from St Martin's Lane in the west to Drury Lane in the east, and from Long Acre in the north to a slightly irregular line behind the backs of the houses in the Strand on the south. At the time of transfer most of the land was pasture its centre portion being enclosed by a fence, later a wall. The parish boundary was drawn just outside the limits of this enclosure following a line which, though historically important, has no obvious mark in the built-up area to-day.[1] It is easier for present purposes to look beyond this line and to regard Covent Garden as being the area bounded by High Holborn, Kingsway, the Strand and Monmouth Street–St Martin's Lane. With some exceptions this is the area which has been considered by planners in the debates over the future of the district following the departure of the market.

This broad definition of Covent Garden takes in a good deal of land outside the Bedford Estate, for instance the property north of Long Acre owned by the Mercers Company and the field further to the northeast called Marshland which was laid out as Seven Dials in 1691. But where the market and the streets immediately surrounding it are concerned, the Bedford family, plus their agents and advisers, played the crucial role from the sixteenth century until the sale of most of the property in 1918. Their involvement, first as developers and then as managers concerned to preserve the reversionary value of the estate, was similar to that of other great landlords elsewhere in London, and like most of them the Bedfords' urban holdings were only part of the family property: they also had land in Bedfordshire, Cambridgeshire, Devon and elsewhere. So through their commitment the history of Covent Garden has a further dimension as part of a family economy bestriding town and country, in which urban revenues could subsidise rural projects and vice versa. In its own way the market, swallowing up farm produce for distribution to London's population, was a daily reminder of these wider links.

FEET 0   100   200   300   400   500   600   700   800   900   1000

METRES 0   100   200   300

The Piazza and St Paul's Church

At the time when the Bedfords acquired their land in Covent Garden the Strand was already built up as a road of suburban mansions linking the City with the court at Whitehall. John Russell moved into one of these in 1539, a house which had been the London residence of the Bishops of Carlisle. In about 1586 the third Earl had built for him a new house on the north side of the Strand where Southampton Street now runs: behind it was a spacious garden whose rear wall was to form the southern boundary of the Piazza development.

Bedford House, as it was called, went up six years after the first of a series of royal proclamations which attempted to limit the growth of London: its completion might be taken as a sign of how easily the earliest of the proclamations could be flouted. The impulse behind these measures was at first a fear of over-population and the consequent problems of food supply, disease and possible civil disorder, but gradually their aims and functions were extended.[2] Queen Elizabeth's 1580 proclamation forbade the building of houses within three miles of the gates of the city where no houses had stood before and limited the number of families per house to that existing. James I in 1605 added an order requiring the use of brick, or brick and stone, in the building of new house-fronts and two years later forbade the building of houses except by special licence. He thus enlarged the scope of building control to cover some aspects of design and opened the opportunity, which his successor was happy to take up, of using a system of licensing or compounding with offenders as a way of raising revenue. However well-intentioned his civic planning ideals may have been, the restrictions that he and Charles I put on building joined the galaxy of complaints laid against the monarchy in the years preceding the Civil War: they were specifically mentioned by John Pym in his *Declaration of the Grievances of the Kingdom* presented to the House of Commons in 1642.[3]

From 1615 onwards the administration of the proclamations was toughened by being entrusted to a special commission amongst whose number by 1620 was the Surveyor of the King's Works, Inigo Jones. He joined in the inspection of building operations and his hand can be recognised in the last of James's proclamations, plus those issued by Charles in 1625 and 1630. In the latter two sanction was given for altering foundations in rebuilding projects to ensure 'Uniformities and Decency': permission for such work could be given by four or more commissioners, 'whereof the Surveyor of Our Workes to be one'.[4]

For the fourth Earl of Bedford to seek the aid of Inigo Jones in the development of the family's Covent Garden estates was not as obvious a decision as it may appear to present-day eyes. It certainly was prudent to involve him, or to agree to his involvement, in a project which so flagrantly contravened the building restrictions, but however calculating the Earl's intentions may have been the partnership was a surprising one. Although the family owed its rise to power to favourable court connections the fourth Earl was more a friend of Pym and his parliamentary associates than of the Crown. From their point of view the works of Jones were not just startling innovations but the chief symbols of the monarch's abuse of power. Did they not include two chapels where catholic rites were observed and the Banqueting House in Whitehall where masques of absurd extravagance were performed? Equally, taking Jones's point of view, it is remarkable that he should set his hand to a scheme which had as its centrepiece a church intended to be run on liturgically radical lines. Such contradictions, compounded by the fact that no records of payment to Jones have been found in the Bedford family papers, lend an element of mystery to the genesis of the Covent Garden plan, though they do not detract from its importance. It is known from other sources that Jones was responsible for the design of St Paul's church and the houses on the north, east and west sides of the Piazza.[5] Whether looked at on their own, or as part of the planned layout, these have long been recognised as buildings of seminal importance.

Neither of Charles's building proclamations referred to licences for development but, being keen to live without parliament, he revived the practice. In 1631 a licence was issued to the Earl of Bedford permitting him to alter or demolish existing buildings in Covent Garden, to divert roads and to put up new buildings in brick and stone. For these privileges the Earl paid £2,000 into the Privy Purse, followed by a further £2,000 four years later when he was challenged for not having obtained a pardon for building works carried out before getting the licence.

The area that the Earl intended to develop fell largely within the walled-off section at the centre of his estate. In the middle of this he inserted the Piazza, a generous open space bounded on the north and east by terraced houses, on the west by the church and two attendant houses and on the south by the wall of his own private garden. Into the square from the east ran Russell Street, lined up axially with the portico of the church, while the opening from James Street divided the terrace on the north side into two equal halves. King Street and Henrietta Street running west from the Piazza formed, with Bedford Street, a built-up rectangle mirroring the open square. The outer edges of the development were completed by what are to-day called Floral Street, Bow Street–Wellington Street and Maiden Lane.

As the term 'piazza' suggests, this layout reflects in its scale and rationality Inigo Jones's detailed knowledge of Italian architecture, particularly in this instance the Piazza d'Arme at Leghorn and its two Parisian imitators, the Place Royale and the Place Dauphine. The idea of a residential square with its church, shared open space and discreet service roads, soon to seem so quintessentially English, was thus in this first instance a foreign import; but in the way it was executed it had a local stamp put upon it. Although sanctioned – if not actively supported – by the king, the scheme was carried out by the Earl with the aid of fifty or so speculative developers to whom he granted building leases. He himself pointed the way by marking out the overall layout, building the church and three sample houses, and laying out some of the foundations of other buildings. Beyond these measures he relied for the control of development largely on articles of agreement attached to the building leases. Numbering ten or more these dictated, amongst other things, the use of building materials, the thickness of walls, the height of rooms and, from May 1632 onwards, the right of the Earl to inspect building plans. The speculators who took leases were not all building tradesmen but those who were included a number connected with the King's Office of Works, notably Issac de Caus and Edward Carter. As well as taking building plots for themselves these men may have helped supervise the whole project on behalf of Jones or the Earl.[6] Such criss-crossing of roles, where the distinction between architect, builder and developer becomes hard to distinguish, was to become a typical characteristic of estate development, as common in its way as the idea of the formal layout.

Compared with many of the squares which followed in its wake the Piazza was grand in its conception, the houses on its north and east sides particularly so. These had four storeys plus attic and basement, the ground and mezzanine floors being concealed behind the 20ft high arcaded walkway. Above the arcading, which was of rusticated stone, a brick elevation divided by pilasters rose to a deep eaves cornice. Behind the uniform facades the houses, seventeen in all, had varied plans though probably in every case the hierarchy between the floors was the same, the third storey with its views across the Piazza being the principal floor. The dignity of the whole composition lay partly in its classical regularity but equally in its generous scale, especially its lofty arcading and broad window spacing. Unfortunately, to appreciate these qualities to-day one is forced to rely on the record of paintings and engravings, for the original fabric was whittled away bit by bit from the early eighteenth century onwards (Figures 2 and 3). What does survive is Henry Clutton's Bedford Chambers of 1877–9, a sensitive attempt to recreate part of the composition on a yet larger scale: its arcading is quite faithful to the Jones design but above that level the similarities are less exact (Figure 67).

St Paul's church has fared much better, though the tinkerings and rebuildings that it has experienced since its completion in 1633 make it impossible to declare all of its fabric genuinely original (Figure 4). Its bold simplicity seemed to contemporaries, as to later generations, confirmation that the Earl threw it up in the cheapest way possible in order to give his estate respectability: as one MP put it in 1657, 'if he built the church it did advance his houses' rents'.[7] Yet in fact the design was less the result of calculated meanness than an attempt by Jones to build a church in the classical idiom suited to the needs of Anglican worship. The temple form and the most primitive of the classical orders, the Tuscan, seemed fit expressions of the spirit of protestantism, especially of the radical strain the Earl espoused. The Earl's beliefs also help explain the striking anomaly that the grand portico facing the Piazza leads to a blank doorway. According to William Prynne, it was intended at first to place the altar at the west end, opposite the entrance under the portico, but the ecclesiastical authorities insisted that the liturgical convention of the altar at the east end be observed.[8] Bar the confusion over doorways this turnabout had few repercussions for within the double square of the church the chancel is set apart by no more than a slight change in floor level; and the portico, denied its proper purpose, has always had a life of its own as the central feature of the Piazza. As seen to-day the church is almost wholly the product of a restoration by Thomas Hardwick following a fire in 1795 and two further treatments in the late nineteenth century, by Henry Clutton (at

2 (facing page, top)
The Piazza, c 1649–56. This painting by an unknown artist is the earliest view of the Piazza yet traced. On the left is the garden of Bedford House with a domed banqueting house in its corner.

3 (facing page, bottom)
Part of Wenceslaus Hollar's mid seventeenth-century bird's-eye view of West London.

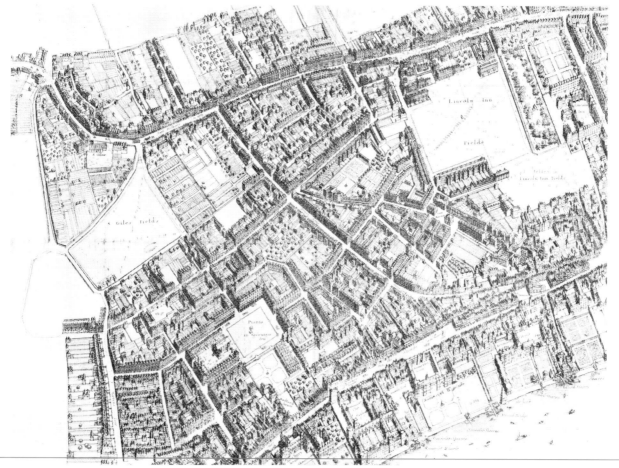

4
St Paul's Covent Garden

the same time as he was working on Bedford Chambers) and A J Pilkington.

The warrant for the Earl's building licence referred to 'houses and buildings fit for the habitations of Gentlemen and men of ability'. Working at a time of strict building control, and in an excellent location, such a booster claim was easily met. The development, completed by 1639, was filled by an aristocratic and upper class tenantry prepared to pay as much as £150 a year for a place in the Piazza. Twenty-five years later, after the hiatus of the Civil War, few of the first residents were still present but the social quality of the area had hardly declined: 7.6 per cent of householders in the parish were titled.[9] But keeping such an illustrious population was harder than getting it, especially once rival developments had started going up further west. In competing with newcomers such as Leicester Square and St James's Square Covent Garden suffered the usual difficulties of the pioneer, not least that changes had begun to seep into the area making it seem less ideal than it once had been: of these changes the casual inauguration of a market on the south side of the Piazza was the most serious.

The Establishment and Growth of the Market

In the laying out of new parts of London each ground landlord sought to reproduce on his estate a microcosm of the whole city, providing within his development for all the essential needs of residents. Amongst the features thought necessary was a market, intended to serve bodily needs as the church served spiritual ones and to produce a regular income from rents and tolls. Set against landlords' expectations was the City which claimed that according to a grant made by Edward III in 1328 it had a monopoly over the establishment of markets within a seven mile radius. In the first half of the seventeenth century the City was successful in using this claim to stave off competitors: in 1636–7, for instance, a plan to set up a market at St Giles-in-the-Fields was defeated in a Star Chamber case.[10] But during and after the Civil War this constraint was broken as a series of markets were founded in the western suburbs: some, like Clare Market, getting well into their stride before they received their charter; others, like Hungerford Market and Brooke House Market in Holborn, officially recognised from the very beginning[11].

The right to establish a market in Covent Garden was not mentioned in the building licence granted to the Earl of Bedford, nor is there any evidence that it was envisaged in the original plans. The first hint that an incipient market was in existence occurs, characteristically, in a note of protest from the City Court of Aldermen in 1649 though it does not appear that they were able to bring it to a halt.[12] In 1656–7 the church-wardens of St Paul's paid 30/- for painting the benches and seats in what they called 'the Markett place'. To rename the Piazza like that so soon was a trifle precipitate for the market at that stage was probably no more than a huddle of traders occupying the space between the low railing around the central area and the wall of the Bedford House garden, a picturesque side feature in the square rather than an engulfing activity. It was though sufficiently permanent by 1670 to be recognised by a royal charter. By this the fifth Earl and his heirs were given the right to hold a market for fruit, flowers, roots and herbs in Covent Garden every day of the year except Christmas Day and Sundays, and to collect tolls from it.[13]

The charter was a crucial document, not simply because it marked the authorisation of what became the major fruit and vegetable market in the kingdom but because in its terms lay the market's future strengths and weaknesses. The area of the market was defined as covering the whole of the Piazza, absurdly adequate as that must have seemed in the seventeenth century, and the commodities to be dealt in were listed: bread, cheese, butter and meat–foods increasingly retailed through shops–were not mentioned, nor was hardware of any kind. No distinction seems to have been made between sales to individuals and to retailers, unlike some other markets which had separate hours for different types of customer.[14] Tolls, the most contentious matter of all, were sanctioned but not itemised by different foods or containers: there was thus a broad leeway for the Bedfords or their market lessees to alter tolls, and for traders to dispute their right to do so.

For the first century and a half of its existence the Bedfords did not run the market themselves but leased the rights to the highest bidder, receiving £5 per annum in the first years rising to £1,200 per annum by the 1740s. The second lessees were allowed to formalise the arrangements in 1677–8 by building a row of twenty-two shops, complete with cellars, against the garden wall. However these did not have a very long life, for in 1705–7 Bedford House was demolished, its site and garden being laid out as Southampton Street, Tavistock Street and Tavistock Row. With its protecting wall gone the market was pushed closer to the centre of the Piazza, a row of forty-eight new shops being built inside the railings. Looking a bit like a row of garden tool-sheds these can be clearly distinguished in pictures by Balthasar Nebot and others; beyond them the north side of the square seems to have been little encroached on in the early eighteenth century (Figures 5 and 6). A further rebuilding of 1748 created 106 more substantial shops set in two rows with room for cart standings between them.[15] The cellars to these shops or their predecessors survived to become part of the vaults beneath the present market building.

The jumble, stink and noise of the market did nothing to preserve the fashionable reputation of the area; rather, it gave convenient cover for the growth of associated activites of a kind sure to drive the last of the good tenants away—coffee-houses, brothels, gaming-rooms and night cellars. Exploiting the fag-ends of leases that no-one else would take these users slipped into old properties, especially in the streets and courts towards Drury Lane and the Strand.[16] 'One would imagine', wrote one reporter in 1776, 'that all the prostitutes in the kingdom had pitched upon this blessed neighbourhood for a place of general rendezvous. For here are lewd women in sufficient numbers to people a mighty colony'.[17] The atmosphere of democratic conviviality in the coffee-houses, about which it is so easy to be sentimental, was offset by the dangers and brutalities of the streets around.

The market itself by the early nineteenth century filled the Piazza with a jumble of carts, baskets, huts and awnings, as much in need of renewed control as its neighbourhood. Traders in 'China and other Crockery Ware, Poultry, Old Iron, and a variety of articles not enumerated in the grant' had intruded themselves, no proper cleaning took place and arguments about tolls were becoming more fractious every year. In an attempt to straighten matters out the sixth Duke of Bedford obtained an Act of Parliament in 1813 redefining his authority. But on the crucial problem of tolls this Act was as vague as ever, referring to 'such Toll and Tolls as is or are usually taken or collected within the said market'. Such ambiguous phrasing drew attention to difficulties rather than solved them, with the result that the years following were bestrewn with court cases over the rights and obligations of market traders.[18]

Through the evidence of this litigation it is possible to assemble a picture of the customs and usages of the market in the period immediately before Charles Fowler's building went up (Figure 7). King's Bench judges needed a patient exposition of the hidden order in the apparently anarchic scene in the Piazza; of how growers and dealers were distinguished, how tolls were collected and how the various sections of the market served different needs. Most of the cases brought by the Duke of Bedford or his lessees were against traders who exploited flaws in the regulations to pay a lower toll. For instance, a market gardener bringing a mixed cartload of produce could pitch in the casualty market for a toll of only 4d but if he separated his fruit to sell in the fruit market at the northeast corner of the Piazza he was charged on each container, generally 2d a barge (a large basket). In the same way, potatoes sold in the potato market, which ran along the south side opposite Tavistock Row, could be rated at 4d or 5d a sack but if included in a grower's cartload they paid much less. To compound confusion, yearly tenants in the long market (running parallel with the potato market) paid no toll at all.[19] For a sharp counsel these contradictions, plus the weak

5 (facing page, top)
The Piazza in c 1717–28 looking north. Engraving by Sutton Nicholls.

6 (facing page, bottom)
View of the Piazza by Balthasar Nebot, 1735.

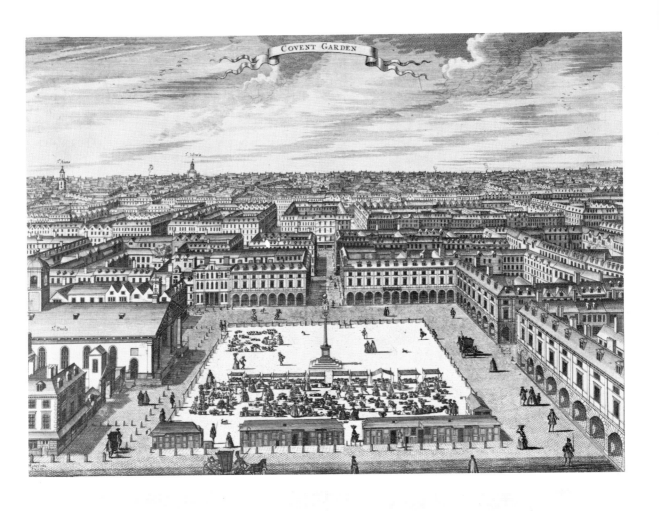

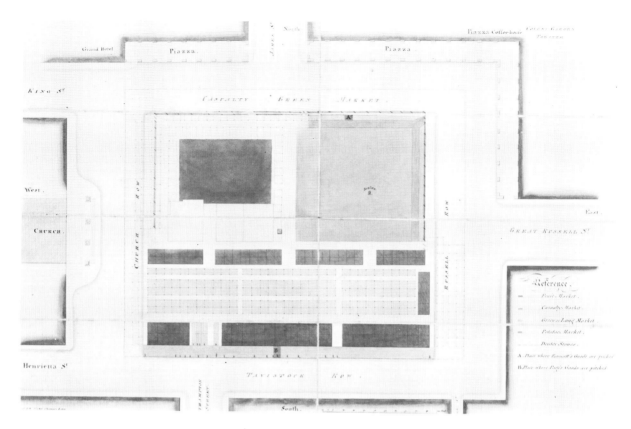

7
Plan of the market probably made at the time of the lawsuit Duke of Bedford v Aaron Emmett, 1819.

wording of the 1813 Act, constituted a sufficient case yet there was still one further line of defence. Within the Dedicated Market, as it was called, china salesmen, bird-cage makers and locksmiths had set up shop, displacing its official functions. A trader forced off his normal pitch, or prevented from getting into the market at all, could point to these trespassers as fair excuse for his defiance of the rules.[20] Listening to such pleas it seemed that only a total rearrangement of the market would settle such discords.

Charles Fowler and the Design of the Market Building

No-one was more aware of the market's problems than the Duke of Bedford's solicitor J H Fisher, who was responsible for preparing cases against offending traders. Conscious that these had the effect of inflaming ill-will rather than eradicating it he wrote to W G Adam, the Chief Agent, in 1826 lamenting that the market showed 'a total want of that systematic arrangement, neatness and accommodation which tends obviously to facilitate business and increase public convenience'. Further than that, he submitted a plan showing how it could be reorganised on the same site to give more space and better cover to its users.[21]

Sympathetic though he might be to such a submission, Adam had to balance it against the hundreds of other calls made on the family revenue. The sixth Duke, who had succeeded to the title in 1802, followed to the

full the extravagant enthusiasms of the age – the collection of classical
antiquities and works of art, the cultivation of exotic plants and new
building on his estate–all of which helped secure the immediate influence of the family, but left his advisers in despair about its long-term
fortunes (Figure 8). Seeing himself as custodian of the interests of future
heirs Adam hammered away at the need for economy, referring con-
temptuously to what the Duke 'fancied were amusements (& no doubt
were in imagination tho' never actually enjoyed)'.[22] With these anxieties
in mind it is easy to appreciate that Fisher's proposals might not have
been taken up without the chance coincidence of a substantial offer of
capital. The Commissioners of Woods and Forests, the government
department concerned with street improvements, offered the Duke
£29,000 for land needed in a project to widen the Strand. This, plus the
sale of another small property, looked like meeting the £30,000 that it
was estimated the new market would cost.[23]

To carry out the work required a new Act of Parliament to replace the
unsatisfactory one of 1813. The Bill, read for the first time in March
1828, described in its preamble the way that existing arrangements had
outgrown themselves to the point that drastic reform was needed.
Details of the proposed new building were given, especially the assign-
ment of different parts to the various branches of the trade. A schedule
of tolls was laid down, more exactly defined than before, and the Duke's
right to make bye-laws was authorised. The principal petitioners against
the Bill were those whom its clauses, and the rebuilding, were designed
to exclude–the china sellers and ironmongers whose presence contra-

9
The lower courtyard at Hungerford Market.

vened the original charter. With only their opposition to overcome the Bill had an easy passage to receive the royal assent in June 1828.[24]

The building plans placed before Parliament were the work of Charles Fowler whose name had been put forward by Fisher in his letter advocating the project. Fowler was born in Devon and served his architectural apprenticeship in Exeter before coming to London in 1814. In the twelve years that followed his works, though not numerous, included the Courts of Bankruptcy in Basinghall Street and his first market, at Gravesend in Kent.[25] He had attracted Fisher's attention as the architect of a scheme announced in 1825 for replacing the worn-out buildings of Hungerford Market, which lay between the Strand and the Thames where Charing Cross Station now stands. His solution to the problem of providing for a market of mixed uses on an awkward, sloping site had a clarity and grandeur which makes it easy to appreciate why his advice was sought elsewhere well before building works there had begun. He saw the new Hungerford Market as having three sections, set in progression from the street to the river: first, a courtyard surrounded by colonnades and shops, with residences on the upper storeys; then a hall occupied by casual traders' stands with galleries above 'somewhat in the manner of a bazar'; and finally a second courtyard at a slightly lower level used as a fish market, overlooked by galleries connecting with those above the hall (Figure 9). On its river front the building was to be terminated by two rectangular bastions containing taverns, linked by a terrace.[26] Straightforward as this plan was, it had great qualities of 'playful picturesqueness' in its changing levels, varying roofline and sequence of closed and open spaces.[27]

Conceived of as a joint-stock enterprise, the Hungerford Market project was halted at its outset by the economic alarms of the late 1820s, with the ironic result that Fowler saw his Covent Garden market finished before the designs which had singled out his abilities to Fisher had begun to be executed. Once it was completed in 1833 Hungerford turned out to be a commercial disappointment, too much of a mixed bag to compete with more specialised rivals.[28] Despite the imaginative attempt to secure trade from the south bank by opening a suspension bridge across the river, it succumbed to the demands of railway terminus building in 1862.

Although W G Adam was keen to keep him at arm's length for as long as possible, Fowler was immersed in the Covent Garden project from the end of 1826 onwards with only the faintest hint that another architect might be employed.[29] His 'beloved first scheme' (as Adam scornfully called it) was drawn up in 1826–7 and exhibited at Somerset House: a model was made soon after which also went on public display. It is a mark of Fowler's talents, plus perhaps his obstinacy, that his original designs survived as the basis of the submission to Parliament and, altered and truncated but not changed in their essentials, that they determined the form of the completed building.[30]

In his plans Fowler had to encompass the varied functions of the market, each well-entrenched in its own traditions: in particular he had to meet the needs of growers and buyers wanting to pitch their produce or park their carts within the market area, and the demands of whole-sale and retail salesmen for more permanent shop accommodation. His first decision therefore was not to build over the whole of the dedicated market area but to provide open space for pitching stands around the margin of the building and in two courtyards within it (Figure 10). The shops were to be housed in three parallel ranges each fronted by colonnades on both sides, linked at either end by broader colonnades with terraces above. The two outer ranges were terminated by square lodge houses, assigned as pubs or coffee-houses, and had at their centre porticoed passageways leading through to the courtyards. The centre range, shorter and broader than the others, had a hall above intended for permanent stands. From this hall, or from staircases in the lodges, it was possible to reach the two terraces which were occupied by the more exclusive retail parts of the fruit and flower markets: heated conservatories on each terrace would enable more delicate plants to be preserved for sale all the year round. The hall and terraces were in fact features which extended the provisions of the market, adding 13,000 sq ft to its area and offering the possibility, through careful policing of the staircases, of attracting 'a more superior class of visitors than can at present venture to approach it'.[31]

If this plan did not have quite the same spatial inventiveness as his Hungerford Market design it did fully demonstrate Fowler's facility in summoning order out of chaos, giving dignity to the pandemonium of market trading. At the same time his list of the materials he intended to use showed him to be sensibly aware of the buffeting the building would have to take, yet ready to venture his arm with new techniques. The columns of the colonnades, which would have to survive endless knocks from carts and waggons, were to be of granite; entablatures and balustrades of Yorkshire stone; all walls of brick except the lower parts of the

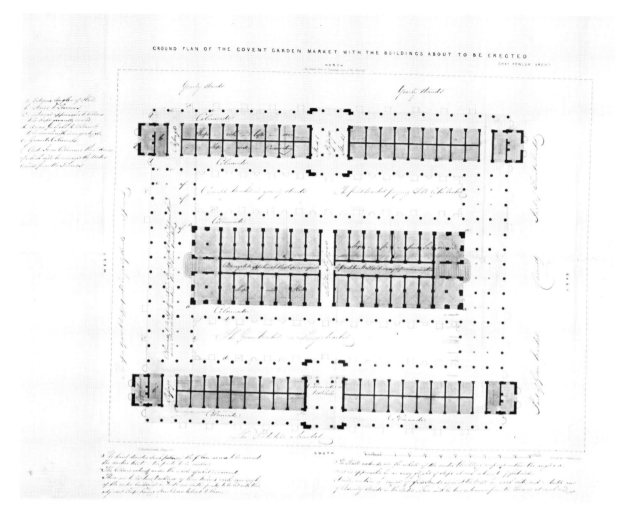

10

Preliminary plan for the market building by Charles Fowler, 1827. At that stage Fowler intended to have cross terraces at both the west and east ends as well as colonnades on the courtyard faces of the three ranges.

lodges, which were to be of granite ashlar. The terraces were to be floored with stone slabs on an iron frame, in part supported by cast iron columns which could do double duty as rainwater pipes. The roof over the hall was to be slated but the others covered with zinc – a material cheap, durable and not easily stolen.[32]

The delay between the completion of the first design and the start of building work late in 1828 was long enough for second thoughts to be had, especially by W G Adam. At his insistence Fowler produced estimates for scaled-down versions of the project, the cheapest omitting the terraces and galleries to the central range (presumably these galleries were themselves an adaptation of the original upper hall idea): but he refused to consider deleting the central range altogether. 'I think Fowler don't deal fairly by any plan he dislikes', complained Adam, 'Let him understand that . . . he must lay himself out to make the restricted plan as perfect as he can economy being always taken into account'.[33] The Duke took an active interest, if not in money-saving schemes at least in architectural details, for instance the shape of the roofs over the outer colonnades and the windows in the lodges (he preferred square to round-headed openings). Once construction was under way he wrote

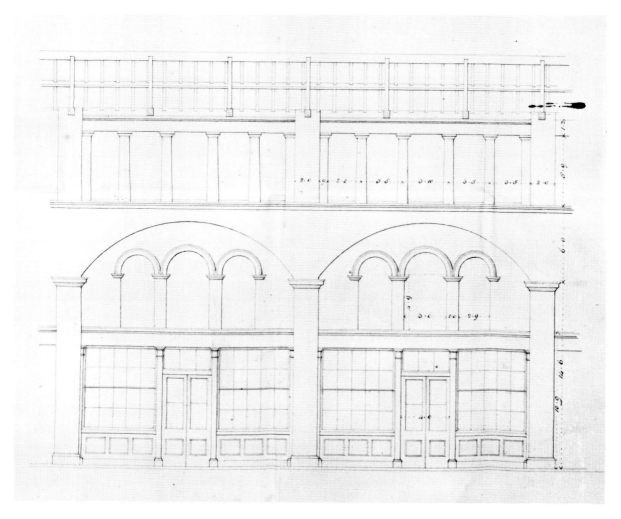

11
Revised design for the internal elevations of Central Avenue.

detailed comments on the drawings for the sculptural group to surmount the east pediment of the central range: 'Mr Sievier's Group is very pretty and well composed and perfectly classical but I think it would be better without the votive Deity which may give rise to observations and discussions'.[34]

Stubborn though Fowler's response to suggested alterations may have been he was unable to see his original designs carried out just as they stood. Probably at the suggestion of George Charlwood, a market official, the colonnades were omitted from the courtyard elevations of the three ranges so as to give more unobstructed space for trading.[35] The central range lost its first storey hall, the ground floor being re-arranged as a top-lit arcade of shops sixteen feet wide (Figure 11). The proposed colonnade and terrace at the west end was reduced to a narrow terrace fronting the central range echoed by similar features in the inner elevations of the other two ranges. This last change in particular destroyed the symmetrical compactness of the first plan but it had the beneficial effect of setting the building back a respectful distance from the portico of St Paul's.

The Completion of the Building

The contract for building the market, which was put out to tender, was awarded to William Cubitt of Gray's Inn Road, who not long before had broken off his partnership with his brother Thomas: this was the first of countless jobs on the Bedfords' Covent Garden estate for which his firm was responsible.[36] The work was carried out in stages with the market apparently continuing to flourish in whatever space was available: first to be completed (by March 1829) was the north range, followed by the south range, the central avenue and finally the east terrace (Figure 12). There seems to have been no official celebration of the start or finish (Adam thought 'Fowler's notion of a ceremony on laying the first stone all nonsense'), the closest thing to an opening day being when the flower market conservatories began trading on June 5th. 1830.[37] Even then there remained much to be done. The fountain intended for the centre of the terrace had been designed but not made, and Sievier's sculptural group was not ready. Not till the following year, with these embellishments in place, did Fowler feel prepared to submit his bird's-eye view of the completed building to the Royal Academy (Figure 13).

The progress of building construction is seldom as smooth as the bare narration of dates makes it appear. In this case Fowler and Cubitt had to contend with last minute changes in the brief—some stemming from traders' demands, others from the Duke's architectural enthusiasms—plus headaches in the supply of materials. Early on, probably before the contract was signed, it was decided to give a more extensive basement and better covering to the fruit market in the north courtyard. Fowler designed a roof extending over the eastern half of the courtyard with semicircular ribs carried on cast iron columns, open at its sides so as to help ventilation: the location of the columns can still be traced in the stone flooring.[38] Once Cubitt had started a further change was imposed, that the upper storeys of the lodges and the portico entrances on the north and south fronts should be of Yorkshire stone, not brick.[39]

The worst problem, not surprisingly, was that of obtaining a supply of granite for the monolithic columns of the colonnades, the facing of the lodges and the pilasters between the shopfronts on the outer elevations. At first Fowler favoured Haytor granite from his home county of Devon but within months he realised that the quarry could not keep pace with construction. Both the Duke and Adam mistrusted his motives for seeking other supplies: 'The Duke said at once you know F is supposed to be in connection with Heytor & he was the advocate for that he cant therefore be for putting other on us. My answer was that the Duke was correct, but it might be Amicus Heytor sed magis Amicus Cubitt.'[40] Such reproaches were overtaken by the need to look for other sources: after toying with the idea of Penrhyn granite, most of the supply eventually came from Aberdeen. However six years after the market was finished Fowler's memory of this crisis had a slightly different complexion: 'After a great quantity of the granite had been provided, the Duke was induced (but not by me) to have all the columns from Aberdeen.' Even if he had never favoured Scottish granite he was wrong in this instance to imply that the switch of supply was an impulsive decision by the Duke late in the day.[41]

12 *(facing page, top)*
View of the market with Central Avenue under construction, c 1829.

13 *(facing page, bottom)*
Bird's-eye view of the market building by Charles Fowler, 1831.

The final cost of the building had to take account of these modifications, plus the embarrassing need to redo parts soon after completion. The paving in the long market and potato market had to be relaid with better curvature to carry off the rain and Fowler's novel zinc roofs had to be stripped off, much to his chagrin, and replaced by lead: he was convinced that the fault was not in the material but the way it had been laid.[42] In addition there were expensive services to be put in. Gas was laid on for all the open parts of the market and central avenue: forty-one lamps, some on brackets others on cast iron standards. Water came from an artesian well 280 ft below central avenue, drawn up and distributed by a steam engine 'on Brathwaite's most improved principles'. Tenants heated their own premises but Messrs. Jones and Co., the horticultural building contractors who supplied the conservatories, were asked at the same time to put in their heating apparatus.[43]

By May 1831 the building had cost £54,312: Fowler, paid at five per cent, had received £2,715. The following year the final figures was given as 'nearly £61,000'; later still the sum quoted was £70,000 'roundly speaking'. All these figures shot well beyond Cubitt's tender price of £34,850, putting a strain on Bedford revenues which the income from their agricultural estates was barely strong enough to take.[44] But in the long term the building proved a sound investment. Bedford Office accounting, though sophisticated for its time, did not venture into the question of what it might have cost not to build it in terms of increased congestion and diminished trade. In a more straightforward way it was calculated that the rise in revenues which followed its completion represented a return of about five per cent. This seemed meagre enough to be quoted as an excuse for not adding to the building in later years, though probably investors in other fields would have regarded such a steady income as quite satisfactory.[45]

Profits apart, the completion of Fowler's building did have the effect, at least for a few decades, of silencing complaints and dispute about the way in which the market was run. The more scrupulous terms of the 1828 Act, backed up by the decision that the market should be managed by Bedford officials rather than lessees, contributed to its improvement, but they might well have been ineffectual without the order that the building established. The success of its layout was that although it imposed regularity on the organisation of the market it did so in terms highly respectful to old usages. Familiar arrangements were maintained within the new setting. Potato merchants returned to the south side of the market, with far more room in the new shops than in the terrace of sheds they had occupied, and far greater cellarage; the fruit market was where it had been before rebuilding as, broadly speaking, were the pitching stands and casual cart stands; the three pubs set up in the south range almost exactly where they used to be. In all, eighty-one tenants moved in of whom only six were newcomers. Rents were higher, but in every instance the Duke's agent felt confident to justify the increase. For instance, the tenants in the south side of central range were 'as near as possible in their former places, with improved premises having rooms above, kitchens below and better cellaring', and Butler's herb shop in the south west lodge (paying £2/3/- a week) had 'as much room on the surface as before – much better rooms upstairs & addl cellarage.'[46] (Figure 14).

14
*James Butler's herb shop in the southwest
lodge, a photograph taken at the end of
the century after the iron roofs had been
added to the building.*

15
*Central Avenue as it looked in the last
years of the market, when all the original
retail shops had been taken over by
wholesale traders.*

16

The east terrace in 1831, complete with the two conservatories and the fountain especially designed for it by Fowler.

Though familiar in its disposition there was nothing humdrum about the building. For those who weren't traders its main impact was in its outer elevations with their austere Greek Doric colonnades, punctuated at the centre of the north and south sides by pedimented porticoes; and in its two areas given over to retailing, the central avenue and east terrace. In the avenue fruiterers' and florists' shops, alternating down each side, created 'one of the prettiest sights in London', an easy lure for those in search of exotic or out-of-season produce (Figure 15).[47] Up on the terrace the two conservatories formed a proto garden-centre for the sale of plants, miniature trees and garden ornaments; the cast iron and glass buildings being themselves an advertisement for the delights of greenhouse gardening. From the terrace the visitor could look back down Central Avenue or out onto the animated scene below (Figure 16). Viewed from that standpoint, or indeed from any aspect, the building appeared to fulfill the prediction of one of the conservatory tenants: 'It will be the best in the world & no one but the Duke would have made it'.[48]

Chapter 2

The Leviathan Nuisance. The Market Under Attack

The most enthusiastic report on Fowler's market building was in J C Loudon's *Gardener's Magazine*. The article (almost certainly by Loudon himself) concluded a description of the building with the forecast that it might represent 'the commencement of a new school of architecture', the School of Reason as against Authority or Progressive as against Stationary. In this rather predictable contest Fowler had attributed to him all the qualities that a radical architectural manifesto might proclaim: he based his designs on 'fundamental principles, instead of antiquated rules and precedents', respected the functions the building had to serve and sought to use the most suitable materials. Obeying these principles he had produced at Covent Garden 'a structure at once perfectly fitted for its various uses; of great architectural beauty and elegance; and so expressive of the purposes for which it is erected, that it cannot by any possibility be mistaken for any thing else than what it is'.[1]

To highlight Fowler's achievement Loudon selected as his example of architectural ineptitude the Bank of England, a building in which he felt the use of columns and other features as mere ornaments left the passer-by unaware of its intended purpose. As a contrast this was almost as insensitive as he accused the architects of the School of Authority of being, for it took no account of the peculiar problem of articulating the blank walls of a high security building. If Loudon had adhered to his interest in function a better comparison would have been with contemporary market buildings completed or planned for other cities.

Looking across the country as a whole London was conspicuous for the size of its wholesale markets–Smithfield for meat, Billingsgate for fish, the Borough Market, Spitalfields and Covent Garden for fruit and vegetables–but equally, its paucity of substantial retail markets of the kind found in most provincial towns. Small general markets established to serve a particular area or estate, like St James's Market or the Fitzroy Market, were fading from existence, and the lesson of Hungerford Market was that the same kind of venture on a larger scale was no more sure of success. As if to drive the point home in the most spectacular way Baroness Burdett–Coutts opened her Columbia Market at Bethnal Green in 1869 with the aim of providing a wholesale and retail trade in a wide range of products as in provincial markets: within weeks it was pronounced a failure–just a few red herring stalls but no buyers.[2] It seemed that Londoners who did not use ordinary retail shops, or were served at their door, preferred the turmoil of costermongers' street markets where informality bred the expectation of an easy bargain.

The first contrast between the Covent Garden building and its equivalents out of London was that they were designed largely for public retailing, a function which Fowler accounted for but did not allow to predominate; and whereas he had to provide space for growers' carts and pitching areas, mostly in the open, they needed as large a covered space as possible. Of equal importance where their development and management were concerned, the major provincial markets were the work of municipal or public enterprise, expressions of a corporate consciousness which London at that time conspicuously lacked.

In the clutch of markets which went up before or soon after Covent Garden the model was set by the St John's Market in Liverpool (1820–22), a project by the Corporation costing £35,000. Its vast, rectangular

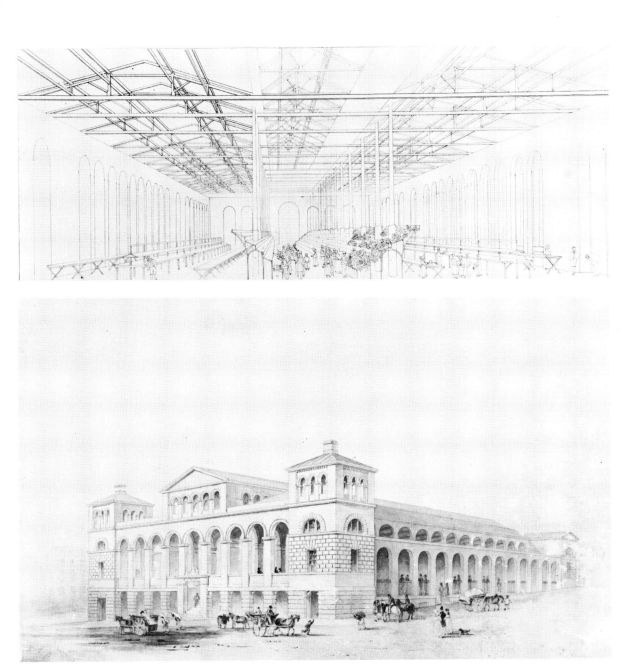

building housed four ranges of stalls under a five-bay roof, with shops
and offices set into the outer walls. At Leeds the Central Market (1824–7)
followed the same pattern – shops for butchers and fishmongers, stalls
for fruit, vegetables and dairy products – with the added bonus of a hotel:
this, though, was financed by a joint stock company with widespread
local support. Birmingham's Market Hall (1835–5) was built by the
town's Street Commissioners who had purchased the market rights from
the Lord of the Manor in 1824. Charles Edge's design provided a column-
ed entrance flanked by shops, leading to a hall divided into three ranges
by the cast iron columns supporting the roof (Figure 17). Finally at
Exeter the Town Council, equipped with an Act allowing them to remove

the market from the street, held a competition in 1834 for the design of two buildings, a Lower Market for corn and meat and a Higher Market for more general produce. Fowler won the prize for the first, George Dymond for the second: following Dymond's death a year later Fowler was asked to execute his designs in addition to completing his own work. Of the two commissions – both of which called essentially for large covered halls – Fowler produced the more subtle solution by dividing his interior into three main ranges with two subsidiary aisles, one of them open towards the street as an arcade (Figure 18); but Dymond was responsible for the most spectacular feature, the main elevation of the Higher Market with its Doric portico and screen.[3]

Considered together these markets had enough common denominators to be regarded as a type. Generally built by public authorities for retail trading, they had straightforward plans and the barest (usually Grecian) embellishment: cast iron (according to Loudon, the most handy weapon in the assault on the Stationary School of Architecture) was introduced where necessary but not put to such dashing use as it was to be later on. Seen against this overall picture the Covent Garden building stands out for its greater intricacy of function and layout and its conspicuous difference in ownership. These qualities setting it apart were, by and large, the ones at the root of its subsequent difficulties.

The Market Criticised

Even the best of architects can see their buildings overtaken by events as uses and demands change, or as new building materials make their designs appear obsolete. To attempt to provide for the needs of mid-Victorian London, dizzy with the pace of its own transformation, was to court the accusation of being out-of-date almost before the mortar was dry even if, like Fowler, you were classed amongst the progressive. The *Building News*, sympathetic to the problem of keeping up with the times, had to admit in a report on the building in 1858: 'If it no longer deserves its old reputation, it is not on account of its own faults, but because the trade has so far grown as to exceed the accommodation, and because we know by experience that better accommodation can be given'.[4]

In the years since the building was finished London's population had risen by over a million, to meet whose appetite suppliers had to search for new sources (especially from abroad) and new methods of cultivation: they also had to serve enthusiasms, such as for flowers and potted plants, which spread with the aestheticising tendencies of the age. Though not connected with any of the new railway termini Covent Garden was ideally placed equi-distant between the most important of them, and close to the major Thames crossings. Being so well placed, the pace of expansion drove it into even greater prominence, not just in London's food supply but as the price-setting market for the nation. In these circumstances it is not surprising that the building came to seem inadequate, or that it could be described at one and the same time as 'one of the prominent glories and the prominent shames of London'.[5]

As much as he did not account for an unforeseen rise in demand, so Fowler did not have the prescience to design a building twenty years ahead of its time. In the freestanding roofs that he built at Covent

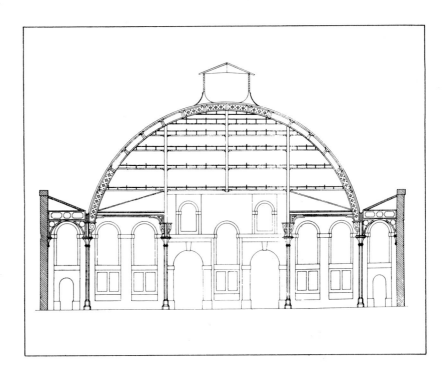

19
Derby Market Hall, section from the
Civil Engineer and Architect's
Journal *1866.*

Garden and Hungerford Market, and even more at his Syon House conservatory, he showed his appreciation of the possibilities of cast iron construction, but they hardly went far enough to satisfy critics who twenty years later had the examples of the first station trainsheds and the Crystal Palace to point to. At first it was Central Avenue which came under attack, appearing narrow and unadventurous (especially its simple king post roof) compared with the glazed arcades going up in Paris and the English provinces. 'Had Covent Garden market been so laid out', wrote W H Leeds in 1841, 'with a central rotunda, having a handsome fountain in the middle, and conservatories forming an upper gallery or arcade over the shops and mezzanines, a very striking coup d'oeil would have been produced, at the same time that the market itself would have been greatly improved as to accommodation and convenience'.[6] That in its turn seemed a tepid solution once the dazzling glasshouses of the 1840s – the precursors of the Crystal Palace – had been completed, or the great crescent truss trainshed roofs such as that at the rebuilt Lime Street Station in Liverpool (1849–50). They put in mind the more radical possibility of roofing over the whole Piazza and its neighbouring streets, a scheme which might (thought its author) come to be appreciated given time: 'What would at first be a mere utilitarian creation of iron and glass, would in time assume an architectural aspect, and become one of the architectural ornaments of the metropolis'.[7]

Any of these projects might have seemed far-fetched had it not been that the mid-Victorian generation of provincial market halls took up the use of cast and wrought iron with gusto. Derby opened its hall in 1866, with a central space covered by a semi-circular wrought iron roof of 81ft span carried on cast iron columns: one of the consultant engineers on the project was R M Ordish who simultaneously was assisting in the completion of St Pancras Station (Figure 19). Coventry Council sought the advice of Frederick Peck, noted for his Agricultural Hall in Islington. He gave them a hall 90ft wide covered by a single span roof supported by coupled columns.[8] Far closer to home, once work started on the Floral Hall at the northeast corner of the Piazza there was one of the most elegant examples of iron construction staring Fowler's building in the face: that example, more than any other, induced the idea of bringing his work up to date.

The Iron Roofs and Other Improvements

Suggestions for the improvement of the building started to flow within months of its opening. In 1831 tenants of stands in the Long Market (as the south courtyard was called) put in the first of many petitions that they might have the protection of a roof like the one in the Fruit Market, 'and that your memorialists will cheerfully pay the additional Rents and Tolls required for the said part of the Market being covered'.[9] In this they were disappointed: indeed, the only alterations agreed to in the first thirty years of the building's life were the erection of a short iron roof to protect the flower stands at the west end of Central Avenue (1839–40) and the extension of the Fruit Market cellars (1846).[10]

By 1860, as the growth of press criticism made clear, something more than a tinkering solution was called for. Charles Parker, the seventh Duke's London Steward, devised a scheme for which he had a model made, intended to enlarge the market area by installing an upper storey in the two courtyards: pitching stands could go upstairs, where they would be properly roofed and lighted, while vehicles were parked below. If, as it would seem, this addition would have left the ground storey courtyard shops in utter gloom it is hardly surprising that it was not proceeded with especially since the market gardeners, who looked like having most to gain, found it 'most objectionable'.[11]

Whatever solution was found, whether as far-reaching as Parker's proposal or not, would have to take account of the existing fabric which was itself beginning to show signs of wear. Before any further action was taken William Cubitt and Co were commissioned in 1871 to give it a thorough renovation – renewing balusters and paving, repairing brickwork and plaster, repainting the woodwork and partly replacing the east terrace conservatories. All of this was respectful to Fowler's design and the firm's work of forty years previously, following the original form and materials, but in two areas Cubitt's were asked to make larger alterations. Shop tenants had generally been allowed by the Bedford Office to make minor modifications to their premises as and when need arose but with Cubitt's on site there was a chance to respond systematically to requests from Central Avenue tenants for more radical changes. All the existing shopfronts there were replaced by new ones containing larger plate glass windows the effect of which, reported the Duke's Steward, was to 'Impart a handsome and improved and more cheerful appearance to this part of the market'. At the same time some of the shops' south courtyard fronts had coiling iron shutters installed. The twelve tenants involved had a total of £126 added to their rents to cover the cost. To improve Central Avenue yet more the windows onto the east terrace and the western balcony had their louvred boardings replaced by casement openings.[12]

As Cubitt's started work the Market Gardeners, Nurserymen and Farmers Association (the main growers' organisation, founded in 1828) were debating the possibility of taking their members' business to the City's Farringdon Market, so frustrated had they become at the reluctance of the Bedford Office to grant them better facilities in the market.[13] At first hearing this dispute sounded like a stereotype case of oppressed traders versus extortionate owners, and that is how the press often reported it, but it had other dimensions which gave it a more entangled character. Growers who used the pitching areas and stands in the open courtyards had to find their own covering for goods and their own lighting (usually a naphtha lamp or lantern) to supplement the rather feeble gas lamps. They had grumbled since the opening that they deserved better protection from the weather, more so since the 1850s when imported produce sold through the market shops began to compete with theirs. A petition of 1852 outlining their complaints (the first of at least six between then and 1873) contrasted their position with that of traders in the covered markets of other cities, referring also to 'the great improvements in the construction for covering Railway Stations . . . by substituting glass and iron as a cheap material'.[14] In failing for so long to respond to their pleas the Dukes of Bedford and their stewards were not displaying hard-headed obstinacy so much as indecision whether to favour the growers' interests or that of other factions in the market. For as fast as petitions for roofing were received rival resolutions came from salesmen and shopkeepers insisting that with a roof over their heads growers would linger in the market all day trying to steal retail trade, and that their rubbish lying about in an enclosed space would be thoroughly unhealthy. Of the two groups, those opposed to the roofs had the power of knowing that they contributed far more to the Duke's revenues but equally they must have realised that if the growers were driven away they would have little left to deal in. By 1873 the determination shown by the Market Gardeners Association had driven a split in the ranks of the shopkeepers which left the ninth Duke free to try the experiment of erecting the first of the large iron roofs.[15]

The art of iron roof construction was sufficiently advanced by the 1870s for endless permutations to be played in the problem of roofing the courtyards. William Cubitt and Co, asked to prepare plans and a model, showed just how various the solutions could be – from a simple 'shed-roof' similar to Fowler's roof in the Fruit Market, running the length of one of the courtyards without touching the existing elevations, to an ungainly triple-pitched structure striding across the entire building: Fletcher Lowndes and Co, ironwork contractors, suggested a semi-circular roof over each courtyard (Figure 20)[16]. The design chosen was for two separate roofs with skylights, supported on cast iron columns set against the walls of the building: the first of these, over the south courtyard, was put up in 1874–5 (Figures 21–3).

Undoubtedly this addition transformed the character of the building and the Piazza. To encourage the maximum ventilation (in answer to the shopkeepers' sanitary anxieties) the roof was carried on semi-

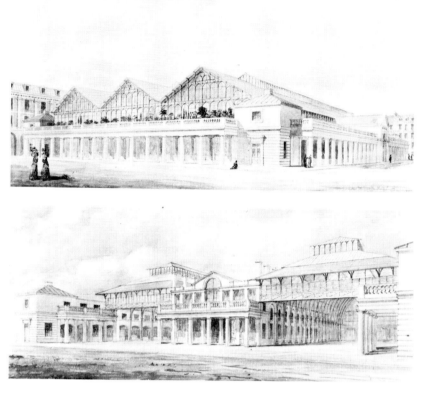

20 *(top)*
Proposed design for roofing the market.

21 *(centre)*
Alternative design for roofing the market. This shows the two iron roofs as built except that the roof over the south (right-hand) hall was not given a louvred screen as shown here.

22 *(bottom)*
The west end of the market, a photograph taken c1876 after the completion of the south hall roof. The roof in the foreground with a corrugated iron covering had been added in 1839–40.

23 *(facing page)*
Interior of the south hall.

circular ribs well above the existing roofs of the ranges, the clerestory between the shopfront wall and the roof being formed by tall round-headed openings. The skylight, which added yet more to the roof's height, had similar openings in it. The effect might have been more over-bearing than it was, for although the roof gave a new scale to the building it was neither oppressive nor disrespectful to the existing fabric. The 2oft cast iron columns followed the rhythms of the shopfront bays, the round-arched bracing between them echoing the first floor window arches of the central range. The impact of the main ribs, painted two shades of light blue, may not have been as ethereal as that achieved at the Crystal Palace but they were at least unassertive, and the roof covering – glass in the upper parts, slates and boarding below – did little to stop the light streaming in. If there might be any complaint it was that the roof was a trifle too plain, with no decoration in the spandrels or cast in the plate iron of the ribs, yet this in itself was in keeping with the austerity of Fowler's original design.[17]

Thrilled to get what they had so long wanted, the Market Gardeners Association took a testimonial of their thanks to the Duke at his Eaton Square home (Figure 24). Then to prove that they were not easily appeased they started within months to petition for the complete cover-ing of the north courtyard. Although designs already existed this was not done till 1889, when the roof erected was the twin of the first except for a louvred screen at its west end.[18]

After the two roofs were up there were few substantial changes made to the building during the rest of its working life as a market. The most important was the replacement of the east terrace conservatories by an office building, starting in 1901–2. Part of the east end of Central Avenue had to be rebuilt after a fire in 1886 and Second World War bomb damage, especially to the northwest lodge, was reinstated with remarkable care.[19] But once the ownership and management of the market began to be seriously called in doubt the building was left to survive as best it could with only minimal repairs. Those who already in the 1870s were discussing its extension, rebuilding or removal would have been amazed to learn that its resilience had to serve it for another hundred years before its rebirth in a new role.

The Other Market Buildings

The completion of the two iron roofs would have seemed a half-hearted response to the demand for more trading space if the Bedfords had not at the same time encouraged the development of the market outside the dedicated area by the erection of subsidiary buildings, a solution open to them through their ownership of the surrounding land. Three extra buildings abut the Piazza – the Floral Hall in its northeast corner, the Flower Market to the southeast and the Jubilee Hall on the south side between the main market building and Tavistock Street. These are best considered in that order though the Floral Hall, first to be finished, came second in the sequence that they were brought into market use.

The title of the Floral Hall, inappropriate for all but a few months of the building's history, is a reminder of the grand aspirations of its developer and the way they were curtailed by the Bedford Office. The

24 (facing page)
Testimonial presented to the ninth Duke of Bedford by the Market Gardeners, Nurserymen and Farmers Association on the completion of the south hall roof, 1876. In the left-hand vignette can be seen the curved glass windows at the end of Central Avenue which have been reinstated as part of the restoration.

To
His Grace
FRANCIS·CHARLES·HASTINGS·NINTH
Duke of Bedford

May it please your Grace.

We the Members of the

Market Gardeners' Nurserymen & Farmers' Association

desire to tender our most grateful thanks for the very great boon
conferred upon ourselves and the P   by the
renewal in of an important portion of Covent Garden Market
and in requesting your kind acceptance of this Address which also to
express our sincere trust that you A are spared to the X
X to witness the successful completion of the undertaking so
pleasingly lent 6 result for the Public convenience.

On behalf of the Members of the MARKET GARDENERS' NURSERYMEN & FARMERS' ASSOCIATION

W   y 6   S

Signed   Edward Haward, President. Decimus Clarke, V. President.
Members of the Committee.
C. W. Alderson.   John S. Gomme.
John Nicholls.   W. J. Robjoit.

March 6, 1876.   Malcolm Searle, Secretary.

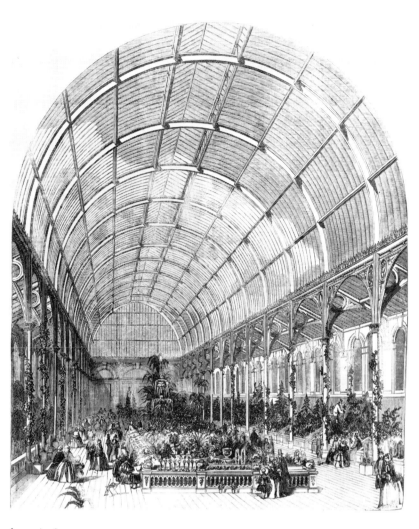

theatrical entrepreneur Frederick Gye, who became business manager of the Opera House in 1848, dreamt of a metropolitan improvement consisting of a gigantic iron and glass arcade on a brick viaduct running from the Bank of England to Trafalgar Square: along its length there were to be shops, cafés, exhibition-rooms and 'an extensive flower market, constructed entirely of glass'.[20] When the Opera House was destroyed by fire in 1856 he sought the chance to realise the flower market section of this scheme on part of the site. He at first planned to place it behind the new Opera House but soon determined on the layout that can be seen to-day with the hall running along its south side. Ninety-year leases for the Floral Hall and the Opera House were signed in February 1857, amongst those acting as mortgages being the architect of both buildings E M Barry, the contractors C and T Lucas, and the seventh Duke of Bedford. Work on the Opera House sped ahead to a reopening in May 1858 but although the Hall had been publicised there was nothing of it to be seen by that date (Figure 25).[21]

The truth was that when it came to executing part of his visionary arcade Gye wanted a cheaper version than the Bedford Office thought suitable for such a prominent site. Acting for the Duke, Charles Parker

26

View of the Floral Hall from the Piazza. On the left can be seen the first part of the offices erected on the east terrace of the main market building.

insisted that the first designs be altered and enriched; that an arched roof should be substituted for a pitched one, a dome added and an impressive entrance made from the Piazza. Gye was perplexed as to 'the possible use of the elaborate dome (which is 104 feet high above the Piazza pathway) with its intersecting arches, to an establishment like a Flower Market' while Barry, torn between commitment to his client and delight at being required to produce something grander, had to admit that these modifications added greatly to the cost.[22] Armed with the Duke's double strength as ground landlord and principal mortgagee Parker carried the day, to be vindicated by the enthusiasm with which the building was greeted when it opened in 1860.

The main axis of the Floral Hall consisted of a nave with arched roof carried on cast iron columns (as Parker had suggested), flanked by two narrow aisles. Over the short return axis towards the Piazza was the semi-circular dome, 50 ft in diameter, topped by a lantern (Figure 26). The arched roofs were expressed on the Bow Street and Piazza fronts in fan-shaped facades carried on round-arched arcades, both having circular decoration cast in their ironwork. Beneath was a basement as large as the building itself, ventilated via flues in the columns above. What was

27
Fruit auction in progress at the Floral Hall, 1913.

described as being 'one of the latest and probably best adaptations of iron to architectural purposes' was delightfully finished in a decoration of grey or lavender walls and white columns, finished off with gilding.[23] The removal of the roof and dome following a fire in 1956, and their replacement by a far more utilitarian covering, is one of the saddest losses there has been to this type of building.

Complaints from developers of being browbeaten by estate stewards were common enough in the nineteenth century but Gye was entitled to protest that his treatment by Parker went well beyond the normal bounds. For once the building over whose design they had fought was completed he found himself in a new dispute with the Bedford Office which lasted for the rest of his life. His intention as stated from the beginning was that the building was to be used as a flower market for which, as he correctly foresaw, there was a much needed demand, but when the time for its opening came Parker opened a rival market at the southeast corner of the Piazza. Despite the offer of bargain rates to traders Gye's scheme was never successfully established (he claimed to be losing 'upwards of £133' a week in 1861) so he turned to other possible uses, especially concerts, only to be frustrated by Parker's claim that these were a nuisance to neighbouring tenants and contravened his lease.[24] Rumours came and went as to how Gye intended using the hall – as a giant café, for skating, even perhaps (so G A Sala scurrilously remarked) for 'exhibiting himself to an admiring public at a guinea and a half admission'. No solution was found till after his death when in 1887 the lease was bought back by the Bedfords and the building converted into the foreign fruit market. The large-scale brokers who dominated that trade soon ranked amongst the highest toll-payers in Covent Garden (Figure 27).[25]

The wholesale flower trade in the market was first carried on at the west end of Central Avenue and under the Piazza arcade just north of there. The decision to expand it on a new site at the other end of the Piazza, which so staggered Frederick Gye, was important as being the first time the Bedfords had promoted trading outside the dedicated area. What started in 1860 as an open market with canvas awnings soon became semi-permanent with iron roofs, which in turn gave way for a more substantial building – the heart of the one seen to-day – in 1871–2. This again was a Cubitt project, designed by one of their employees William Rogers, and the ironwork of its main hall had many similarities to the roof they were soon to erect on Fowler's building. In its structure and detail this ironwork seemed to the *Building News* 'especially worthy of notice', but even more so the entrance facade on Wellington Street with its tall semi-circular arches beneath a stone balustrade: 'There is in it nothing particularly striking in the way of originality of design, but there is an absence of that affected quaintness which finds such apt interpretation in the hands of some of the violent Gothic men of the present time'.[26]

As it stood in 1872 the Flower Market had almost 300 stands, most of them let to annual tenants but on the understanding that casual traders could use them when the regulars were not there. Even with this doubling-up system the market rapidly burst its bounds leaving 'a whole neighbourhood . . . literally choked up with flowers', stretching

28 (*above*)
The Tavistock Street elevation of the
Flower Market, watercolour of
c1884–6. The covered passage and
offices on the left were not built.

29 (*right*)
Interior of the Flower Market in the
last year of market trading.

down Wellington Street as far as the Lyceum. To try and halt this out-flow another 100 stands were added in 1884–6 by making three extensions to the building, the most important being a new frontage on Tavistock Street (Figures 28–29). A further block at the corner of Wellington Street and Russell Street was attached in 1904–5.[27]

Such recurrent building activity reflected the anxiety of the Bedford Office that portions of the market might slip out of their hands by operating beyond the district where they had the power to collect rents and tolls. Having, as they thought, met the demands of flower traders and foreign fruit merchants they were caught for the third time in the 1890s by the expansion of foreign flower imports handled by commission salesmen in warehouses outside their area of control. To serve this trade the third of the additional market buildings around the Piazza was built, the Jubilee Market. Like the Flower Market this started as a temporary structure on the south side of the Piazza where Tavistock Row had stood, turned into a fully-fledged building by Lander, Bedells and Crompton in 1904. Unlike its predecessors this had distinct ground and first floor trading areas, with lifts between the two, the ground floor being open-sided. In style it followed the classicism favoured by the Bedfords, though with the Baroque enthusiasms (expecially its little corner domes) typical of its date.[28]

The Sale of the Market and After

Criticism of the market and its buildings, whether by architectural journalists or traders, easily stretched to questioning the role of the Bedford family as owners. After the apparent tranquility of the mid-Victorian years, when even in Covent Garden disputes did not have the litigious character of earlier decades, the last part of the century saw a renewed hostility towards aristocratic property and power. In particular the grip that large landowners had on certain cities through leasehold ownership and other rights, normally granted centuries before the urban expansion from which they were profiting, seemed utterly incompatible with the growth of municipal powers. As one writer on Covent Garden asked in 1871, 'Of what practical value is local self-government when one of its chief duties is left in the hands of a landed monpolist like the noble Duke?'.[29] Markets were conspicuously an area of public welfare best entrusted to municipal enterprise, as most of those in provincial cities were. To pinpoint the anomalous position of towns with aristo-cratic markets, or ones where the market rights were leased at profit, the radical MP Charles Bradlaugh obtained a parliamentary return in 1886 on the administration of markets around the country and subsequently, armed with that information, instigated a Royal Commission on the subject. This investigation, plus other inquiries made at about that time, yielded fascinating evidence on the condition and management of Covent Garden half a century after Fowler's building had opened.

The considerable expansion of trade and growth in the market's area had not been met by any notable reorganisation (Figures 30–32). In the main building there were still the same divisions as defined in the 1828 Act: pitching and cart stands occupied by growers paying annual rents, casual stands rented on a day-to-day basis by growers or salesmen, and

30 (facing page)
Market porter.

shops (usually with offices and cellars attached) held on weekly tenancies by salesmen. Tolls were paid by all vehicles (normally 1/- a waggon, 4d a cart) or produce except when brought in by growers with yearly stands.[30] Yet within this system two important shifts were occurring. In the first place, although there were a large number of tollpayers, a few stood out from the rest in the size of their turnover. In 1891 737 individuals or firms paid tolls, of which 33 accounted for nearly two-thirds of the payments. The top four consisted of three firms of auctioneers in the Foreign Fruit Market and George Monro, a salesman dealing in most branches of the trade.[31] Secondly, two sections of the market were going into decline. Growers whose market gardens were being pushed forever further out by suburban building tended increasingly to entrust their goods to commission salesmen rather than attend market themselves: in 1888 only 32 of the 45 stands allotted to them were taken up. At the same time the retailers in Central Avenue were beginning to feel the competition of West End stores as their fashionable mid-morning trade dropped away.[32]

Labour in the market – the endless trotting to and fro between carts, stands and shops – looked the same as ever but was entering on a transformation as significant in its sphere as the growth of large firms. Almost a thousand porters could find work in the market – more at the height of the soft fruit season, far less in winter. They were paid a weekly wage plus a sum for the amount carried (totalling an average of 30/- to 45/- a week), or a casual sum for each 'turn' or delivery made. The system of licensing them was never tight enough to prevent the market from being a prime target for the thousands who tramped London every day in search of work, sometimes doubling the pool of men and women from which traders could draw. The first steps in decasualisation were made at the time of the 1889 London dock strike when a porters' union was founded which succeeded in persuading the merchants in the Floral Hall to employ only its members: not till well after the First World War did similar restrictions reach other parts of the market.[33]

Watching over the market were twelve Bedford officials (a superintendent, seven collectors, an office clerk, a head porter and two attendants) and seven policemen hired from the Metropolitan Police. If, as was often claimed, one of their problems was heavy drinking amongst the casual porters their lot may have been slightly eased by the closing of the three pubs in the market (the 'White Horse', the 'Green Man' and the 'Carpenters' Arms', all in south range) and their conversion into potato merchants' shops.[34]

The recommendation of the Royal Commission on Market Rights and Tolls in 1891 was that local authorities should be granted powers to take over privately owned markets, if necessary by compulsory purchase. As John Bourne, the ninth Duke's Agent, had informed the Commission in his evidence, such a policy was not anathema to the Bedfords who had for some time been wanting to relinquish themselves of Covent Garden. In 1874, when the Market Gardeners Association were pleading for adequate roofing, the Duke had told a deputation that he was willing to 'proceed with such improvements of a patching and cobbling nature as the existing structure would admit of but if more extensive reconstruction was wanted he would consider selling the market and surrounding

31 (facing page, top)
Asparagus stall in the south hall.

32 (facing page, bottom)
Pea shellers at the market.

properties to the principal arm of London government, the Metropolitan Board of Works.[35] A further bout of criticism of Bedford management followed in the early 1880s, led by *Punch* in its description of 'Mud-salad Market' as 'a disgrace to London' and 'a Leviathan Nuisance': the mood in the market became more belligerent as disputes over tolls and the allocation of space revived. Tired of such headaches, the Duke made his promised offer in 1882–3, first to the MBW and then to the City Corporation. Both balked at the thought of taking on such a troublesome beast and turned it down.[36]

Outside London the last of the major aristocratic markets passed from the hands of their owners before the end of the century: Huddersfield Corporation acquired its local markets from Sir John Ramsden in 1880, Sheffield Corporation finally came to an agreement with the Duke of Norfolk over theirs in 1899.[37] The ninth Duke of Bedford had insisted that however generously he might be tempted he would only sell to a local authority, not a private speculator. But such adamance was not easily sustained as the family found themselves caught between the increasingly ferocious attacks on the parasitical position of large landowners–culminating in Lloyd George's budget of 1909–10–and the persistent shyness of London's government to accept responsibility for the market. By 1913 political rumours of the possibility of leasehold enfranchisement or the compulsory purchase of property without compensation were so rife that the eleventh Duke was advised to look for a private sale, even one involving a substantial long-term loss. There followed a series of feverish negotiations which kept the press of the day agog. The first agreement to sell–not just the market but the whole of the Covent Garden Estate–was made with Mr H Mallaby-Deeley, a 'well-known speculator in land and house property' whose obvious intention was to resell almost immediately at profit. His offer was of £2 million, a third of which was to be paid by March 1917 while the remainder was held on mortgage to the Duke at $4\frac{1}{2}$ per cent. However this deal was not completed, superficially because of a dispute about the legality of the initial agreement and the question of who should retain the Bedfords' private boxes at the Royal Opera House and the Theatre Royal Drury Lane, but more probably because the Duke mistrusted Mallaby-Deeley. Instead a fresh agreement was made with Sir Joseph Beecham (of the famous pill firm), acting as the nominee of a syndicate of Manchester businessmen. This in turn did not run smoothly, for in the hiatus that occurred with the outbreak of war, followed by the death of Sir Joseph in 1916, a private company called the Covent Garden Estate Company Limited had to be formed to fulfill the contract. It was to that firm that the Duke conveyed his Covent Garden properties and market rights in 1918.[38]

The transfer of the market out of the hands of the Bedford family, momentous though it seemed, was only really a sideways step leaving the new owners in very much the same position as the old ones. There remained unresolved the twin problems of whether the market should be handed over to a public authority and how it should be reorganised to meet the changed conditions of trade. On the first, the new company (whose interests were more in real estate than market management) offered to sell the market to the London County Council in 1920, only

33
Interior of the New Covent Garden Market, Nine Elms.

to be given the same refusal as the Duke received in 1883. As regards its organisation, a Ministry of Food Committee reported in 1921 that the market was 'altogether inadequate to the necessities of the trade'; its buildings were obsolete, badly lit and quite unsuited to handling motor transport. In the evidence the committee heard it was frequently suggested that the only solution was a move to a totally new site, or a drastic expansion within the existing area. George Monro Jnr spoke directly to the point: 'It has been the feeling for years that the church is not necessary. It covers a very large area and I should say it is very nearly as large as the so called market. . . . Then there is the Opera House and we think that ought to be moved'. Whether it shared such a cavalier attitude to the surrounding buildings or not, the company was prevented from carrying out large-scale reconstruction of the market by its having sold off many of the neighbouring properties. On the other hand, when it put forward the idea of building a new market at a site owned by the Foundling Hospital a mile or so to the north it was cried down by outside opposition.[39]

It was not till 1962, almost a hundred years after the ninth Duke had first raised the idea, that the market was taken into public ownership. The Covent Garden Market Authority, set up by an Act in 1961, acquired the market buildings and a few adjacent properties for £3,925,000.

It was required as a first priority to tackle the problem which had so frustrated previous owners, the improvement of market facilities. The firm of management consultants appointed to study its possible relocation condemned the existing premises in the same terms as the government committee of forty years earlier and recommended that the market be moved to Beckton in East London. Ideal as this site might have been in some respects, it would not have suited the market workers most of whom live in South London. The Authority therefore took up an alternative offer of a tract of land straddling the main railway line at Nine Elms. There a completely new set of buildings were constructed, designed by Gollins, Melvin, Ward and Partners, ready to receive the market when it finally moved out of Covent Garden in November 1974 (Figure 33).[40]

A simple outline of the decisions leading to the market's move can barely conceal how wearisome the debate over its conditions had become. Stretching over a hundred years the same theme recurs of the search for a competent authority to sort out its inadequacies and muddle. While committees reported on matters already well known and suggestions were made that had been heard many times before the chaos in the market multiplied – a delight for those who enjoyed its picturesque anarchy yet monstrously inefficient. But within the bureaucratic in-decision there was one blessing: because the reform of the market was so long delayed it was not rebuilt on its Covent Garden site, nor when the move finally came was there much doubt that the best of the buildings it left behind should be preserved.

Chapter 3
The Restoration

Nowadays, when there is so much public sympathy for the preservation of historic buildings, it is tempting for the description of a particular project to assume its rightness or inevitability. To make such assumptions may help carry the story along, like any history which pursues a just cause without looking to left or right, but in so doing it may conceal dilemmas and conflicts which properly should be included. In the preservation of any building there are generally four problems, each of which can be treated separately though in reality they most often occur in unison. Should the building be kept or demolished? If kept, how should it be restored? Who should be responsible for the restoration? And once restored what new use (if necessary) should the building be put to? Any of these questions, or combinations of them, point to conundrums which even in the most deserving or straightforward cases need to be resolved.

In a number of respects Fowler's market was more fortunate than most buildings whose future is thrown in doubt. A market is not like a firm which can be declared bankrupt overnight or an institution which may suddenly have to shut down for want of support. If its trade is well-established the closure or removal of a market demands a great deal of forethought. At Covent Garden it was known for at least ten years that the building would be vacated when the market moved out, quite sufficient time for the crucial questions about its future to be solved. Furthermore, by the time it had definitely been decided that the market should be relocated support for the retention of such a building was reaching a new pitch. The reaction to the ruthless way the fabric of British cities had been treated in the post-war period, reinforced by the feeling that there was very little quality or delight in much new architecture, focused in the early 1960s on the appalling and unnecessary demolition of two buildings: the Euston Portico and the Coal Exchange in Lower Thames Street. Stung by these losses – in both instances of buildings only marginally younger than Fowler's – preservation societies were sharper, and public authorities a bit wiser, about the treatment of similar cases.[1] The fact that the Covent Garden building had been listed in 1958 did not put it totally beyond threat, but it did mean that a good first line of defence existed before the debate about what should become of it ever began.

Yet even if the tendency was in favour of retaining the market building the preservation argument had its own enigmas, ones similar (though possibly more complex) to those that occur in any such project. Put simply it was a question of what should be restored, whether an architectural or historic unity should be reinstated or whether instead each accretion should be allowed to remain. At Covent Garden this dilemma was more entangled than usual because the building could not be thought of apart from its setting at the centre of a layout of immense historic importance. At the furthest extreme it could be argued that the market was an intrusion on this layout and that the opportunity was now at hand for recreating the Inigo Jones design in its entirety. This might have produced the finest architectural solution but only through a quite ruthless restoration which would have obliterated many fine buildings, not least Fowler's market. Pondering the same kind of problem in church restoration George Gilbert Scott once remarked: 'The great danger in all restoration is *doing too much*; and the great difficulty is to know *where to stop*'.[2] If it was considered that reinstating Jones's work was 'doing too much', and that the market should be kept for both its aesthetic and historic merits, the same problem of assessment recurred at another level. Should it be restored to its original condition of 1830, or should each alteration and addition be respected as part of the patina of its life? Where in its history should the line be drawn?

When nineteenth century architects debated the ground rules for restoration they were thinking mainly of work on medieval churches where their commissions never called for a drastic change of use. The architects of more recent projects, though haunted by such earlier deliberations, have had to accept tougher circumstances, above all the need to convert buildings to new functions and in so doing to meet increasingly intricate demands for building safety. With such commissions a restoration ideal, whether pure or eclectic, is bound to be tempered by necessity. One of the interests of the Covent Garden project is that because it was so long anticipated there was ample opportunity for the discussion of more philosophical points before blunt realities took over.

The Decision to Restore

Because the market had spread well beyond the area first assigned to it discussions about what should happen in the aftermath of its departure were forced to consider much more than the purpose-designed market buildings. So from the start the future of Fowler's building was tied up with the wider issues of what kind of a place Covent Garden was going to be and who was going to take over the properties owned by the Market Authority and individual firms. These issues, which by the very nature of the place and its traditions were bound to be contentious, assumed a symbolic importance in a yet wider debate about the methods and ideals of urban planning: decisions made and scrapped, policies put forward then reversed, received such attention that those who were not in the thick of the debate were easily confused. To abstract from these arguments the single topic of the treatment of Fowler's market may slightly distort their focus but it is in many respects a subject deserving separate consideration. In particular, it needs to be emphasised that there has been a continuity of policy towards the building which sets it apart from the disputes that have affected so much else in the area.

From the first outline proposals for replanning Covent Garden it was almost always thought that Fowler's building should be preserved. In 1964, before the Bill sanctioning the removal of the market to Nine Elms had passed through Parliament, a London County Council Town Planning Committee had been alerted to the fact that 'an exceptional opportunity would be presented for replanning a key area of Central London'. The same planning report, which was to be used as a framework for later decisions, suggested that the market building and the Floral Hall offered 'interesting possibilities for retention' – hardly strong words, but enough to direct attention to the buildings' importance.[3] The planning team for the area set up by the Greater London Council (as the LCC had become), the City of Westminster and the Borough of

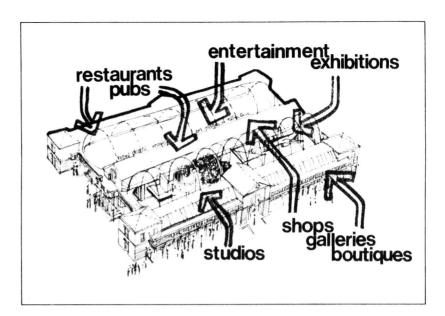

restaurants
pubs

entertainment
exhibitions

shops
galleries
boutiques

studios

34
*Scheme for the market building shown in
the 1968 Draft Plan for Covent Garden.*

Camden completed its first draft plan in 1968. By then the future of the
Floral Hall was less certain in view of proposals for the expansion of the
Opera House but the market building had secured a definite position in
the plan as 'a lively centrepiece containing restaurants, speciality shops,
and galleries opening onto covered arcades'. It was to stand mid-way
on a 'line of character' leading from Leicester Square to Lincoln's Inn
Fields along which were gathered many of the other buildings thought
worthy of preservation. Nothing more precise was said about its use and
treatment but the illustrations to the plan showed the courtyards within
the building covered by modern roofs with a plastic covering, not (as
they are now) by the late Victorian iron roofs (Figure 34).[4]

In confirming that the building would be retained the draft plan set off
the next stage of the preservation debate, the question of what form the
restoration would take. Such is the nature of local government that the
two main disputants to emerge were both part of the same organisation:
the Covent Garden Joint Development Committee which supervised
the making of the plan, and the GLC Historic Buildings Board which
had the authority to comment of any developments affecting listed
buildings. At first the Board took a more radical view of the restoration
than that expressed in the draft plan. Though the plan showed respect
for the historic fabric of the area by identifying 'lines of character' it
emphasised that even in those areas there might be 'controlled renewal'
with 'new buildings sympathetically designed': it was intended that the
market building should have new buildings on at least two sides of it. The
Board took as its priority the reinstatement of the Piazza as a historic
layout. It suggested that the square might be enclosed (especially on its
north and east sides) by arcaded buildings to an Inigo Jones or Clutton
design and Fowler's building altered to fit in with the scale of such a
scheme.[5] One of the drawings made to demonstrate this historicist
solution was slipped in as a supplement to the revised draft plan published in May 1971 (Figure 35).

Following the Public Inquiry into the redevelopment scheme, which

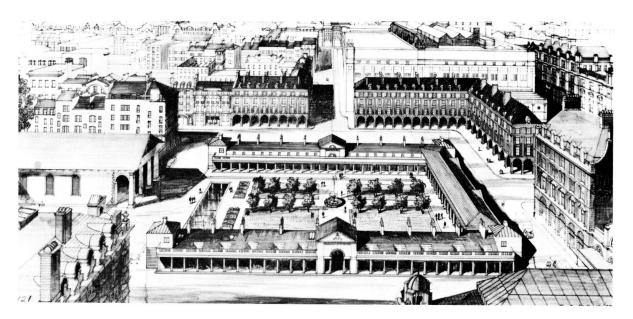

35
Perspective drawing made in 1969 showing a possible treatment of the market building and Piazza. The terraces on the northeast and east sides of the Piazza are shown rebuilt in the style of Henry Clutton's Bedford Chambers.

took place in July–September 1971, there was a hiatus while the decision of the Secretary of State for the Environment was awaited. During that period the restoration of the market building, which had not been a matter of dispute at the Inquiry, began to be looked at in a more matter of fact way as a problem on its own apart from the wider question of the treatment of the Piazza. That is not to say that the debate went at one leap from heady speculations about the reclamation of the Piazza to humdrum talk about cubic footage and fire prevention, for there were still some quite fundamental dilemmas about the work to be resolved. The most important of these, upon which much else hung, was whether or not the iron roofs should be retained. It is hard to think of a better example of the kind of conflict over the limits of restoration which can arise in such a project. The purist argument, put forward by the Historic Buildings Board and for a time accepted by the planning team, was that the building should be returned to its original state minus the roofs: further than that, it was suggested that colonnades might be erected on the courtyard faces as Fowler had intended in his 1827 design (Figure 10). The virtues of this solution were almost entirely architectural, that it would create a building more sympathetic to its setting especially in relation to St Paul's. It could not be claimed that it would be cheaper for the cost of erecting new colonnades, even using a modern substitute for Fowler's granite columns, would probably have outweighed the expense of repairing the iron roofs. The opposing 'roofs on' argument had more ingredients to it: that rather than detracting from the building the roofs gave it added substance, that they were as much a part of its history as the original structure and that their retention would create large, covered halls for public enjoyment. If screens were provided to enclose the halls at either end they could be made as attractive as the gallerias of Milan with dining-out areas, exhibitions and free-standing stalls for small traders.

No-one could honestly insist that they had no say in this debate for it went on for more than a year and embroiled a number of GLC com-

36
*Model made by the models section of the
GLC Architect's Department.
This illustrates the proposal to construct
colonnades on the courtyard elevations
of the building following Fowler's 1827
design and to reinstate the two Tuscan
churchyard gateways that had been
removed in the late nineteenth century.
On the terraces above the colonnades are
the short dividing walls that would have
enclosed small gardens for the flats that
were at one time proposed for the first
floor.*

mittees, conservation societies and interested members of the public who
went to see the model demonstrating the proposals on display at the
planning team's offices in King Street (Figure 36). The Georgian Group
followed the Historic Buildings Board line. They stated that 'the Cubitt
additions did not seem to be of such outstanding architectural quality
as to justify their retention if there was a real possibility of creating the
original building as Fowler originally intended'. By contrast the Victorian Society, true to its historical territory, voted for the retention of
the roofs. Most of the public response was in favour of keeping the
roofs, with comments added such as: 'There is only one answer if
people are to be attracted to use the area – retain the roofs and keep out the
rain'. That, broadly speaking, was the view of the Covent Garden
Development Committee which decided at the end of 1973 that the roofs
should stay put.[6]

To many it seemed that this argument about the restoration was
premature when it was not yet settled who was going to own the building
and carry out the work. The GLC was under no legal obligation to buy
and manage the Market Authority properties and, as anyone could have
predicted, there were a number of other organisations eager to take on
one or more of them. There appears though to have been an underlying
assumption from an early stage that the Council would retain a close
commitment in the area: only delays in obtaining planning permission
prevented their making these intentions explicit. During the period of the
roofs debate other questions about the treatment of Fowler's market

were gradually settled. First, in response to an application from the Architectural Association for use of the building it was decided that it would be wrong for it to be taken over by an institution, or indeed by a single occupier of any kind. From then on there was no danger that it would be run by a multiple retailer as a superstore with a historic setting.[7] Secondly, it was announced at the same time as the verdict on the roofs was given that the GLC would definitely take over ownership and management control of Fowler's market though it was not until some months later, in July 1974, that the final agreement was reached with the Market Authority over the purchase.[8]

The pace of events in the year or so before the departure of the market was such that it is hard to keep their significance in perspective. A particular course had been driven the end result of which was that the GLC was to be responsible for the work, the Covent Garden Development Committee acting as client and the Historic Buildings Division as architects. The broad principles of the restoration had been agreed but the question of how the building was going to be used had only been partially settled. Conversely, a number of things had not happened. The building was not going to be torn down, nor was it going to be sold or leased to a commercial developer. The architectural commission was not assigned to a private firm. The project could have taken many different directions but in the absence of any exactly comparable restorations it is hard to say what the consequences might have been. It is difficult though to imagine that any organisation other than an experienced public authority could have sustained a project of such unexpected complexity.

The Restoration Problem

While the building was still in market occupation, and well before the decision to purchase it had been made, the Historic Buildings Division made a complete survey of its fabric (Figures 37–40). It was hard before their work was completed for anyone to appreciate fully the problems that its restoration would involve. Clambering between barrows, packing cases and the iron cages erected in the halls to protect traders' goods, it was easy on first inspection to see that most of Fowler's original design survived. The two iron roofs, the offices on the east terrace and the alterations that had been made to Central Avenue in 1871–2 were also equally obvious. It was much harder to fathom what went on behind and below the more visible parts of the building. Because tenants had been allowed to make their own alterations, each shop though superficially similar to its neighbours invariably had its own peculiarities: two or three shops were sometimes pushed into one, staircases ran up and down at different points and the treatment of shopfronts, services and finishes was completely unpredictable. More disconcerting still was the fact that the building was really like an iceberg with a high proportion of its accommodation in basements running under about three-quarters of its area; some connected with the shops above but some, especially under the east terrace, independent of them. Stuffed with old boxes, market equipment and the leftovers of use as wartime air-raid shelters, these vaults and cellars were as varied as the spaces above them. The area that they contained would be essential to the building's new use though converting

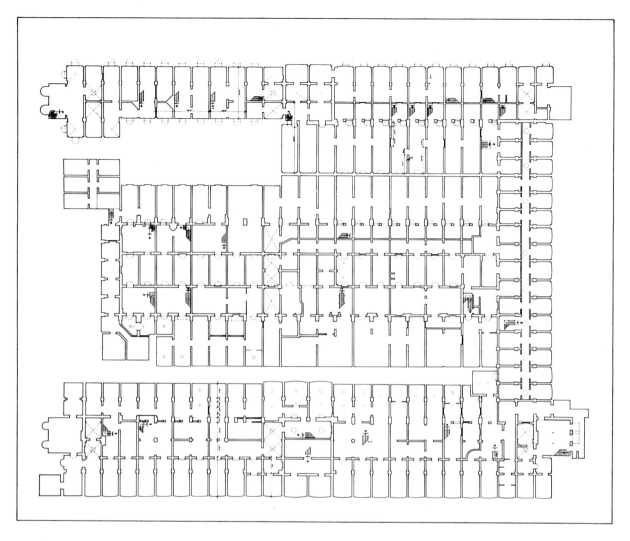

37 *(above)* and 38 *(facing page)*
Basement and ground floor plans before restoration.

them, and making proper access, appeared to be one of the most intractable problems.

During the decades of procrastination about where the market should move to there had been no incentive for anyone to carry out more than minimal repairs and repainting. It is hardly surprising therefore that early inspection of the building revealed, in addition to its hidden intricacies, that many parts of the fabric were worn out: much of the sandstone was decayed, the roofs to both the ranges and the halls needed attention, and structural problems had arisen from the making of ill-considered alterations. Once the market and its clutter were gone it was possible with the help of photographic working drawings to pinpoint the parts most needing attention (Figure 41).

But beyond the fact that so many features called for repair the building carried a yet more awkward legacy. In the Act which had sanctioned its construction the market had been exempted from the London Building Act of 1774 largely, it would seem, to preserve its formal clarity by omitting the necessity to extend party walls through the roofline. The same exemption continued in force throughout the nineteenth century and

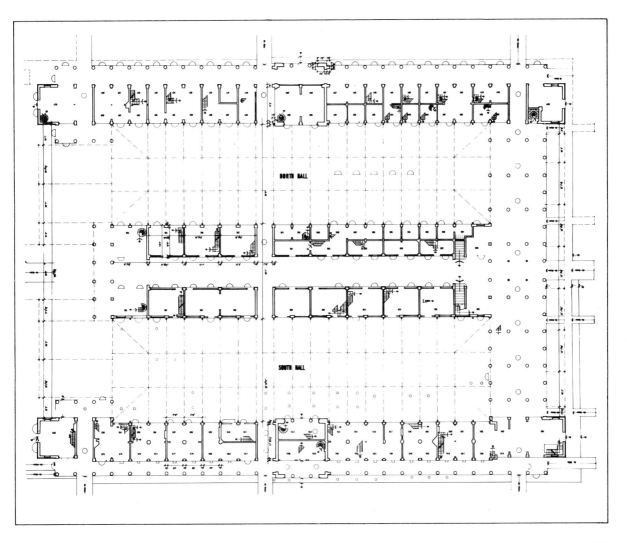

was restated in the 1939 Building Act.[9] However it applied to the building only as long as it was in use as a market so in its conversion to a new use it was forced for the first time to meet the standards for safety and fire protection laid down in the Acts (in particular, the requirements in Sections 20 and 35 of the 1939 Act). In the enforcement of these standards yet another branch of the GLC, the Building Regulation Division, was drawn into the project.

There was plenty in the layout and materials of the building to give anxiety to those alert to safety hazards. Obviously the basements, though not in themselves particularly combustible, could be a lethal trap if fire broke out especially since they had no proper smoke outlets. Fire Brigade officers could still remember how impossible it had been to tackle the fire that raged for a day and a half through the basement of the Flower Market in 1949.[10] In the ranges above ground the main danger lay in the large amount of exposed woodwork: timber floors and staircases, matchboarding and wooden shopfronts. A fire which broke out in one shop unit might easily spread to its neighbour or to the separate accommodation above. In Central Avenue it was even possible for fire to leap

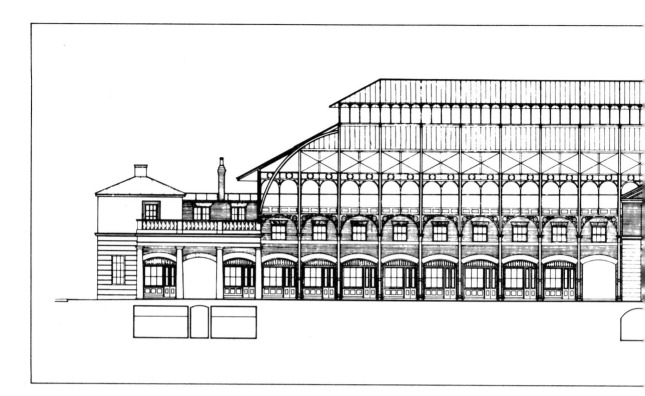

39 *(above)*
Longitudinal section through the north hall looking north, showing the building as restored.

40 *(facing page)*
Central pavilion, south range, section looking south. This pavilion may have been designed for use as a formal entrance to the market.

across the narrow passageway to the shops opposite, or up into the timber roof: that may have been what happened in the fire of 1886. To the layman it may have seemed that the human risk was small in the above ground parts of the building because people could escape into the north or south halls but in the view of the Building Regulation Division they could still be vulnerable there. The columns supporting the roofs, hugging close to the shopfront walls, were of cast iron, a material which if heated and then suddenly doused with cold water can become brittle and fracture. Even given the promise that the columns would be protected, and that no enclosing screens would be erected, the halls were still looked upon as being part of the interior space of the building.

Enough has been said to indicate that the work about to be started was bound to stretch the term restoration beyond the definition given it by Dr Johnson: 'The act of replacing in a former state. To give back what has been lost or taken away.' True, the first motive for retaining the building was that it should be appreciated, if not as it originally was then at least as it was once the iron roofs had been added, and the architects intended that the repairs should be as faithful to what had gone before as possible: that much was certainly restoration. But the second half of the problem, the conversion of the building to a new use, brought with it constraints and demands never imposed on it before many of which were hard to reconcile with the primary aims of the project. Seeking agreement half way seems to many to be as good as defeat, but looked at the other way around it represents double victory. The pragmatic solution reached at Covent Garden, testing each new requirement against the claims of historical veracity, enabled the building to be kept in a way that was not degrading to its past yet which gave it new life and attraction.

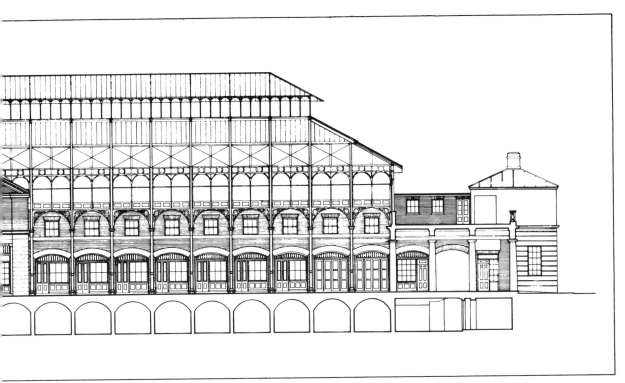

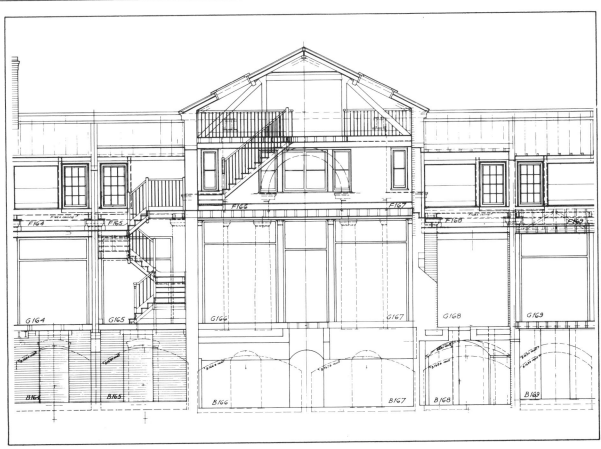

CUT OUT 2 N° IRON CRAMPS
AND MAKE GOOD

DISMANTLE & RESET
CORNER STONE OF CORNICE

CLEAN OFF STAIN

NEW STONE

REMOVE CLIPS AND MAKE
GOOD AFTER

NEW STONES

. NEW STONE

REMOVE SCREW & CLIP
& MAKE GOOD AFTER.

RAKE OUT NEXT CEMENT
POINTING TO PAVING (APPROX 6 m)

DISMANTLE EXISTING STONE
COPING AND REBUILD

NEW STONE (ALSO ON RETURN FACE)

ON RETURN (WEST) FACE
NEW CORNICE STONES
1 × 800mm LENGTH
1 × 1.0 m LENGTH

VARIOUS PLASTIC STONE REPAIRS

NEW STONE

NEW STONE

REMOVE CLIPS AND
MAKE GOOD AFTER.

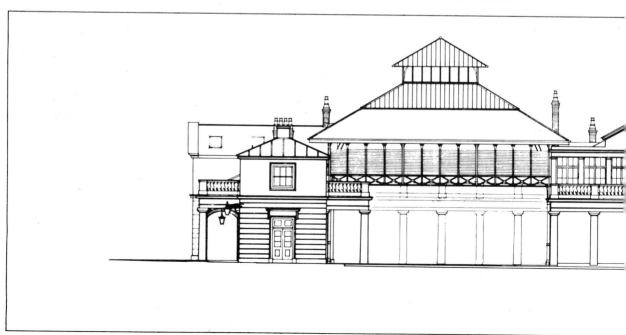

The most fundamental alteration called for was devised as a solution to the two most critical problems in the building's re-use: what to do with the basement areas and how to create enough lettable space to bring in a reasonable rental income. Because the shop space above ground was deceptively small in relation to the total area of the building there was a strong incentive to find ways of bringing the basements into retail use. The alternative of sealing them off (except for essential services and perhaps lavatories) would have brought a saving in building costs but a loss of a quarter of the estimated annual income. The first realistic scheme put forward was to scoop three courtyards out of the basements, one in the north hall and two in the south, making in effect low-level arcades to complement the ranges above. Broad access staircases would help solve the basement fire hazard. The shops in the lower courtyards could either be linked to those at ground level or let as separate units. This inventive proposal appeared to take care of the two major head-aches, not to mention the problem of what to do with the embarrassingly large spaces in the halls. But since it would have altered the character of both halls it was decided to reduce the scheme to two linked courtyards in the south hall, around which (it was first thought) there could be twenty-two small specialist shops (Figure 42). Once this was completed the total lettable space in the basement – the courtyards plus the usable areas under Central Avenue and the north range – would be 30,132 square feet, about 56 per cent of that available in the building as a whole.[11]

Digging a rectangular pit in the midst of a building would not normally be thought of as restoration. In this case, brutal though it sounds, it was the most logical way of changing the function of the building while doing least damage to its original fabric. It is impossible to pretend that the hole is not there, like the concealed steel bracing in a cathedral spire, but equally it does not detract from the overall impact of Fowler's design.

41 *(facing page)*
Photographic survey of the northeast lodge and part of the north colonnade showing repair notes.

42 *(below)*
West end of the market. The section on the right shows the lower courtyard created during the restoration (the line of this section is indicated in Fig 56).

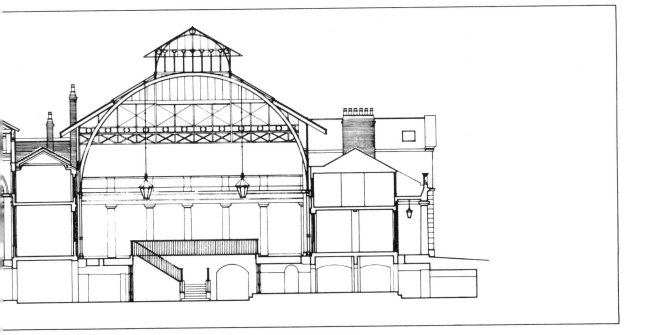

The Organisation and Progress of the Work

The pressures to start and finish as speedily as possible which are present in any building project recurred at Covent Garden. They were given yet more urgency by the feeling that the Council, which had been bombarded with criticism over its intervention in the area, should be credited with doing something that met with general approval; that contractors should be got onto the site as soon as possible to prevent vandalism from setting in and to show that something was happening at last. Set against the desire for haste was the wariness that came of knowing that the success of this project was crucial to the future of Covent Garden, and that the Council would be expected to set a particularly high standard in its work.

The way the work was organised had a commonsense logic to it. There were three main contracts. The first was to partially strip the building, remove unnecessary additions and make a start on the restoration. The second dealt with the iron roofs, work which required a great deal of scaffolding and so was best taken separately. The third and largest completed the restoration and conversion work, including the making of the two courtyards and the installation of new services. The fitting out of the shops by tenants dovetailed with the final stages of the third contract.

The only initial anxiety that this sequence provoked was that the building would be out of use, and so out of public attention, for a long time. The alternative, which was debated in 1974 before work began, was to phase the final part of the work so that temporary uses could be slotted into some of the ground floor units. It hardly seemed that a short let in part of a building site would be very attractive to anyone (or very lucrative to the Council) and it would have undoubtedly impeded the restoration. Indeed, now it is known how many ramifications the project had it is easy to confirm the wisdom of the decision reached that there should be no short-term occupants.[12]

Sanction to start the project by inviting tenders for the first stage was given in June–July 1974 as the final agreements over the purchase of the building were being made. So the first contractor, Walter Lawrence and Son Ltd, was able to be on the site within weeks of the market's departure at the end of the year.[13] The first tasks were the least glamorous though they brought the rapid benefit of revealing the building as it had never been seen in this century. At the west end opposite St Paul's a low iron and glass roof across the front was removed, together with a small office on the balcony at the end of Central Avenue. The iron cages were taken out of the two halls, giving a sense of their spaciousness and the quality of their paving. The offices on the east terrace were demolished and the parts of the balustrade that were missing reinstated (Figure 43). It was hoped at that time to find money in the project to rebuild the two conservatories and the fountain on the terrace which had been such acclaimed features of the original design: meanwhile some of the granite columns supporting the terrace were cleaned and the two east pavilions restored to give an early demonstration of what the end effect of the whole scheme would be. Stage one was finished by the end of 1975 at a cost of £78,000.[14]

43
Demolition of the offices on the east terrace.

44
Skylight of the roof to the north hall under repair.

The work on the iron roofs followed almost immediately and lasted till September 1976 (Figure 44). Until they could be properly inspected it was hard to assess how much attention they would need. In fact they had survived astonishingly well, requiring only local repairs (discussed further below). Fresh glazing was put in where necessary, a temporary rainwater disposal system was installed and the old paintwork was stripped off – all twenty-four coats of it – to be replaced by the original light blue colouring. The contractors for this stage, which cost £113,000, were W J Simms Son and Cooke (Southern) Ltd.[15]

The substantial results of the first two stages could easily be seen, even by those who could only catch a glimpse of the works over the hoardings, but in many ways their most important outcome was a better understanding of the building – the condition of the 700 or so different spaces in it and their interconnections, the secrets that had been hidden by dirt and accretions, and the mysteries of the drains and other services. But as more was learnt so more appeared to need doing in every aspect of the work – restoration, conversion and bringing the building up to an acceptable safety standard – and as each month passed building costs rose. By the time the scaffolding was coming down from the iron roofs it was uncertain whether the third and most ambitious stage could be completed as first intended.

In January 1975 it was estimated that expenditure on the final stage might be in the order of £1,267,000. More precise estimating, plus the effects of acute national inflation, brought the final estimate on the proposed scheme to £2,200,000 by September 1976. In the face of such a racing increase every kind of economy was considered. Parts of the restoration could be omitted, including conceivably the basement courtyards, or the work could be phased so that no more was completed than was originally estimated for, while the rest awaited more prosperous times. At two further extremes, work could be temporarily stopped or, in the belief that inflation could only get worse, it could be speeded up by employing more than one main contractor. In practice the options were not nearly so wide as these suggestions implied for the restoration had already been begun on certain assumptions which would have been wrecked if the first plans had been reversed. For instance, the idea of phased opening bore the same difficulties as the earlier proposal for temporary lettings, that retailers would be reluctant to join a half-finished enterprise. And to abandon the basements would have scuttled the hope of a reasonable revenue return. Squeezed between rising costs and a powerful wish to see the restoration successfully completed, the Covent Garden Committee made what was probably the most satisfactory compromise: that the work should go ahead as planned though minus a good number of details such as the fountain on the east terrace and the grit-blasting of the basement walls. As compensation it was decided that the restoration of the shopfronts should remain in the contract rather than (as was also suggested) being left as the responsibility of the incoming tenants. With these changes the revised estimate for the third stage was £1,958,000.[16]

The final contract, to which the first were both overtures, had two nasty setbacks at its very beginning. Although the tender for the work from F G Minter was accepted in March 1977, no progress could be made

45 (facing page, top)
Making the lower courtyards in the south hall, July 1977. In the dug-out section can be seen the end wall of the basements to the central range and part of the foundations to the basements of south range.

46 (facing page, bottom)
Work on the lower courtyards nearing completion; November 1979

till a government moritorium on capital expenditure was lifted in June that year. Then within weeks of Minter's coming on site – when some further stripping-out had been done and a start made on excavating the lower courtyards – the firm was taken into receivership.[17] It was fortunate that such a calamity came at the beginning of the contract rather than later on when more subcontractors had been taken on and materials ordered, but that didn't stop there being plenty of anxious faces the day the news came through. In the event, the contract was reassigned remarkably quickly to Myton Ltd who have been able to see it through to completion in spring 1980.[18]

The work carried out in the third stage, though stretching over almost three years, does not lend itself to narrative description. Items which in any new building project have to follow in strict sequence have been tackled simultaneously or even in reverse order: for instance, repairs to the exterior stonework and the roofs of the ranges have run concurrently with the renovation of the first-floor rooms and the installation of new services. It is easier therefore to consider the work by topic, highlighting matters which are most likely to arouse the interest of anyone visiting the building. The exception to the rule, where the project has followed the logic of new construction, has been in the making of the two lower courtyards which has been a connecting theme in the final years of the restoration (Figures 45–6). After the lifting of the paving in the south hall (most of which was kept for repairs elsewhere) the basement vaults were excavated: some of the hard core went to fill the original well beneath Central Avenue. The exposed ends of the truncated vaults down either side of the dug-out spaces were finished with brick piers and reinforced concrete arches which, until they were rendered, looked very much like an experiment in 1960s modernism. Staircases with York stone steps were made down either side of the central reservation separating the two courtyards and a further two flights, with granite steps, slotted into the south range. Towards the end of the contract, before the shopfitters arrived, the shopfronts with their granite plinths were put in and the steel railings around the edges of the courtyards fixed. All in all, the work required in the courtyards was perhaps not as extensive as might be thought, mainly because the shops leading off them did not have to be made from scratch but were formed from the vaults beneath the building: even now that they are occupied no-one is likely to be deceived about their origin.

Restoration Techniques

The pressures which compelled the building of the basement courtyards repeated themselves on a small scale in almost every feature of the restoration. The requirements of the building's new use, and of contemporary safety standards, reached to even the minutest details with the result that the straightforward practice of conserving or renewing what was already there was seldom sufficient. Where it could not be achieved the kind of reconciliation with new demands that was sought had to be inventive or even sometimes deceptive, concealing the insertion of safety materials within the original fabric or accurate reproductions of it. At worst not even deception was possible and the new

47
*Column in the north hall under repair.
The two braces, which had been fixed after
it was damaged by bombing, were removed
once the repairs had been completed.*

treatment forced upon the building remains quite evident. The problems
encountered are best considered according to the materials dealt with:
ironwork, stone and brickwork, and woodwork.

The cast and wrought ironwork in the roofs nowhere required total
replacement though sections did need repairing. The iron fixing studs
holding the glazing in the north hall roof needed renewing and one of
the trussed girders which tie the ends of each roof had to be strengthened.
Only one of the cast iron columns supporting roof had any major faults,
a crack resulting from bombing during the Second World War. This was
literally bound up on the spot, using metal wedges which were then
welded into the surface of the column (Figure 47). But work on the roofs
did not stop at repairs, for to protect them against fire two measures were
necessary. The first, which was simple enough, was to insert asbestos
boarding at intervals in their timberwork portions. The second, much
more troublesome, was to cover the columns in some way (in a new
building they would have had to be encased in concrete). The material
chosen, called intumescent mastic, can be applied to ironwork in a rela-

48
*Cast iron columns in the north hall,
the one in the foreground treated with
intumescent mastic.*

tively thin layer which when affected by fire expands like a rising cake to
keep the heat away from the vulnerable part. As used on the columns it
has the virtue of not obliterating the shape of their mouldings though
some of their sharpness has undoubtedly been lost and the fibrous texture
of the mastic, even when hidden under paint, feels nothing like the cast
iron it is protecting (Figure 48). This therefore is a conspicuous example
of a technique which the trained eye will easily spot and perhaps, despite
its use, find offensive.

Along with the ironwork of the roofs the steel railings and staircase
balusters of the lower courtyards deserve to be mentioned. Ideally these
would have been made of cast iron to a nineteenth-century pattern but
again safety considerations intervened. This time the fear was that the
cast iron might be too structurally weak to withstand the press of an
excited crowd. Though not out of keeping, the steel substitute (even
with its nice mahogany handrails) can hardly conceal its businesslike
function.

The treatment of the stone and brickwork was more remarkable for
its extent than for any special technique used. The exterior brickwork,
the stonework and the granite columns were all cleaned by grit-blasting.

49
Stone-carver at work on the coronet above the Bedford coat of arms, central pavilion south range.

With the granite this did little more than strip off the surface grime but with the stonework it revealed for the first time differences of texture and colouring which at some point in the building's history had been covered by a uniform coating of cement wash: it also showed how extensively the sandstone had been patched up with cement and concrete which in no way matched the pinkish-buff colour of the original.[19] For the brickwork the use of grit-blasting, which is liable to destroy the face of bricks, was determined by the anxiety that the preferred method of cleaning with water might saturate the basement walls. As it is, most of the brickwork exteriors are under cover and therefore not likely to suffer from corrosion if they have by any chance been damaged.

The stonework called for more far-reaching repairs than at first thought. The need to renew balustrades where they had been destroyed to make way for additions was obvious, as was the desirability of replacing in stone the parts which in the past had been repaired in concrete (Figure 49). Less conspicuous was the work required under the east terrace, where some of the stone beams had to be renewed or reinforced, and more detailed surgery elsewhere. The central pavilion of the south range is a good example of a feature which has demanded a great deal of

attention: the replacement of some of its ashlar facing, the repair of other surfaces with 'plastic' stonework and the carving of a new coat of arms to go in the pediment.[20] Here the conventional ideal of restoration – making good the existing fabric, substituting new for old only where absolutely necessary – has been carried out to the full.

The best of the work on the building, like the stonework repairs, has been so reticent that given time and weathering it should be impossible to recognise just what was done. It will quickly be taken for granted. The same can hardly be said of the shopfronts. Though they too have been restored or replaced with the same kind of sympathy, and should therefore merge with the total architectural effect, they are utterly conspicuous when set against the general character of shopfronts elsewhere. Throughout the shopping streets of London and other cities there are exceedingly few retailers, whether occupying purpose-built nineteenth-century premises or not, who have held back from the cult of the big plate glass window and the modern fascia. The importance of the Covent Garden shopfronts is not just that they avoid that cult but that they bring the language of Fowler's design to the parts of the building which everyone is most aware of. They are integral to the architecture and an advertisement for it.

The freedom given to market tenants to make their own alterations meant that few of the original shopfronts survived intact. Where they did it was easy to see that although there was a variety of types they all followed a common language (Figure 50). Most had double-hung sash windows set above a stall riser: in some cases both windows could be let down behind the riser and a flap folded over them to make a market stall. Beside the opening was a single or double door and spanning the top of the whole fitting was a glazed cast iron grille. Both the windows and the doorways were recessed to allow shutters to be inserted when the shop was unoccupied. Because of the Cubitt renovation of 1871–2 the shopfronts in Central Avenue were of a quite different character with much larger panes of undivided glazing: at each end of the avenue were traces of special curved windows which used to mark the entrances to it.

Thirty-five of the shopfronts that were in the building when the market moved out had enough of their original features to merit retention: five shopfront frames or frames to the cast iron grilles were also kept. Over half of the survivors were in Central Avenue where they only needed cleaning, and a small amount of rearrangement to improve access to the first floor, before being put back into use. At the same time the curved glass at the corners was reinstated. Elsewhere, in the case of openings that had lost their original fronts and in the lower courtyards where a whole new set of openings had been created, there existed the problem of making suitable new designs. Because no complete set of Fowler shopfront drawings survived these could not be based precisely on original information but had instead to be interpretations of as much evidence as was available. Seventeen new designs were made, some to be used only once or twice in situations which presented special problems, others repeated many times over as was undoubtedly the case with the original shopfronts when the market was built (Figures 51–53). In addition there were drawings made for doors and coverings concealing things that Fowler never dreamt of such as the transformer chamber and the fire

50 (facing page)
Early shopfront on the north side of south range.

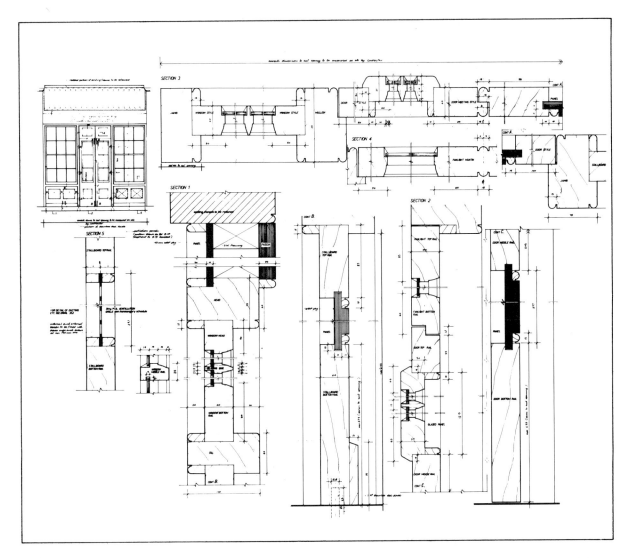

51 *(facing page)*
New shopfront installed in the central pavilion, north range.

52 *(above)*
Working drawing for the shopfront shown opposite.

alarm panels. Each design is as faithful as possible to the original form and style. Windows and doors are again recessed within the shopfront frame, the panels have the same incised line decoration and the iron grilles have been re-used or new ones made. The only significant deviation (made at the insistence of those responsible for letting the shops) is that in most cases the glazing is simpler than Fowler's: the north side of the south range is unique in having had a complete set of twenty-four pane windows reinstated.

In some instances the design of shopfronts and doors had to incorporate materials required by fire regulations. Those forming the entrances to the four staircases in Central Avenue have half-hour fire resistance, and the doors to the compactor room a one-hour fire resistance.[21] To meet these requirements asbestos linings have been sandwiched within the panelling and a special type of 6mm glass used. Only the eagle-eyed will notice that in the windows that have this glass the glazing bars do not support it but stand in front of the pane as pure decoration.

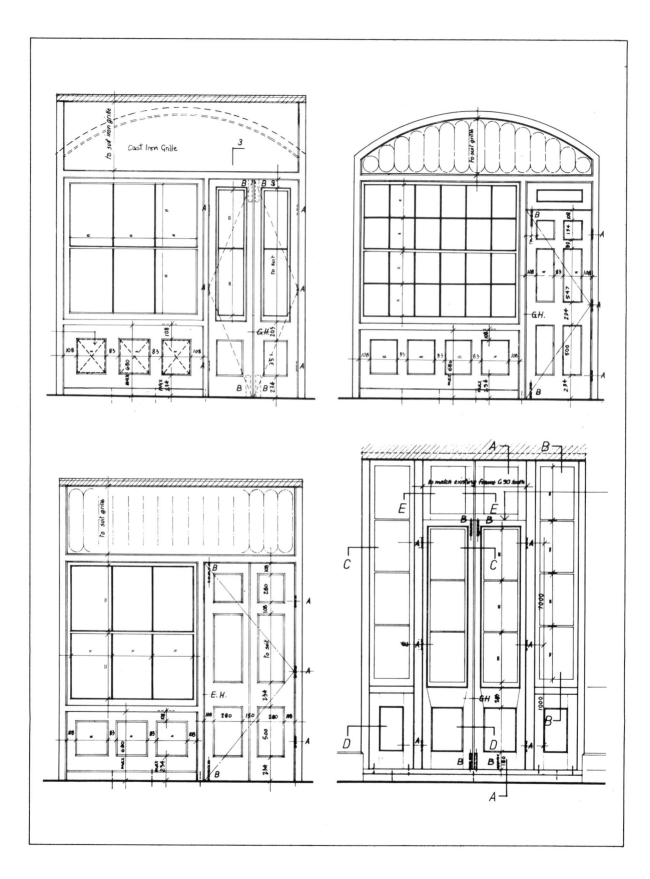

53 *(facing page)*
Four shopfront designs.

54 *(above)*
The new lamps being made. In the foreground is a lamp of the kind that hangs in the colonnades, in the background one of the lamps for the halls.

Services

The conversion of the building has demanded a complete renewal of all its main services. None of these have been easy to fit in but since most are hidden away beneath the building or within its walls they have not produced the same kind of problems as the more conspicuous parts of the restoration. No-one need know that a completely new set of drains has been installed, or that there is a new electricity system with its own ducts running through the basement and a transformer tucked away at one end of the lower courtyards. Only the special perforated chimneys, designed to match the originals, announce the ventilation needed for the gas heating in the first-floor rooms.

But two of the services are not so discreet. The necessity as part of fire protection to put sprinklers in all the rooms could not possibly be solved in a way that would go unnoticed. Whereas a new building can be designed with them in mind, concealing much of their piping, drenchers and sprinkler heads within the fabric, adding them to an old building can only be obtrusive especially if they are made from a set of prefabricated parts. In this case, even when painted to match the surfaces they cross, they are bound to stand out as reminders of the constraints the restoration has had to comply with.

The lighting in the public areas is conspicuous in a much more pleasing way. Here, as with the shopfronts, there was adequate evidence of what the nineteenth-century fixtures looked like but far from enough surviving examples to rescue for re-use. So new lamps had to be designed and made, fitted for electricity rather than the original gas supply (Figure 54).[22] There are four main types: small, square lanterns which hang under the colonnades, straight-sided octagonal lamps in Central Avenue, big splayed octagonal lamps surmounted by golden pineapples in the two halls and round lamps on brackets in the lower courtyards. The first three types are made of copper which with exposure should turn a dullish brown: all are glazed with plastic rather than glass, and those which hang low enough to be whacked by a reveller's umbrella have a special reinforcing inner framework.

Chapter 4
The Building's New Use

In a restoration project such as this, where the end product is not just the preservation of a historic monument but a building enjoying a new use, there is bound to be a balance of interests. If for its part the restoration has to bear constraints required by the change of function, so the new activity put into the building has to be successful enough to ensure its continued survival. A wrong choice of use, or indecisive management, could leave the building in a worse state than before work started – doubly unloved because the first enthusiasms resulted in failure. In the case of Fowler's building the expectations put upon its new use have been particularly high. The hope has been that by prospering in its new role the market will not simply benefit itself but help in the revival of the whole Covent Garden area.

The debate over what should happen to the restored building has been in some ways yet more fascinating than the debate over the restoration itself because there have been fewer precedents to draw on, let alone any thing as authoritative as a theory of building re-use. When work at Covent Garden began it was difficult to think of any earlier examples of building conversion similar enough in character to be helpful. As it turned out, though there may have been few precursors a number of schemes with quite close resemblance to this one were in progress or came to completion in the period covered by the project. All have been manifestations in one way or another of the same upsurge of interest in preservation, the desire to rejuvenate familiar places rather than tearing them down and starting again. Some of the parallel cases are British, notably the revival of the Piece Hall in Halifax with shops installed in the cloth traders' offices, but most are in America: Ghirardelli Square and the Cannery in San Francisco, Trolley Square in Salt Lake City, the Faneuil Hall Marketplace in Boston and others. In each instance as at Covent Garden a historic building has been re-used for retailing, with an emphasis on small quality traders rather than large multiple dealers.[1] There are now sufficient examples of this kind of conversion for them to have acquired their own descriptive term amongst developers and estate agents – 'speciality centres' – and there are early signs that some elementary rules for their success (hardly grand enough yet to call theories) have been formulated.[2]

Although the decisions about the new use of Fowler's building have been largely based on its peculiarities of design and location, with little reference to other projects, it may be helpful to get an outside perspective by comparing it with one of the American schemes. So this chapter, after describing the way in which the building has been filled and making a short detour to discuss the re-use of the Flower Market, concludes with an evaluation of the similarities and differences between the work at Covent Garden and the restoration of Boston's Faneuil Hall Markets.

The Evolution of Letting Policy

Given that the favourable notices the building originally attracted emphasised how ideally suited it was to its function as a market, it might have seemed rash to try and change its use in any way. Indeed once it became imperative to consider what its future would be after the market had gone it was realised that it had many features that were going to make its conversion singularly difficult. All of them can still be easily recognised on looking round the reopened building. The greatest problem, as already emphasised, was the huge basement area stretching under almost the entire building – good for storing vegetables but hard to bring into public use. Coming above ground, the layout is almost equally awkward. On the one hand the four ranges (the two outer ranges plus the two that make up Central Avenue) are extremely narrow with entrances on both sides of each shop unit – again, ideal for market trading but less feasible for other purposes; while on the other hand the two halls are quite wide and so difficult to fill with activity.

It also needs to be underlined that the amount of lettable space in the building is really quite small, even when considered as a total figure regardless of the complexity of the layout. Taking the ground storey and basement, including the lower courtyards but excluding the two halls, the total space available is just under 41,000 square feet. That is hardly more than a single high street multiple store might occupy or, to use a high-flown example, about five per cent of the retail floorspace at the Brent Cross Shopping Centre in North London.[3] Such a comparison is not meant to imply that the building would have suited any multiple retailers – everything in its scale and plan is the antithesis of their ideal – but it does emphasise the limits to what could be achieved regardless of the constraints that respect for its fabric imposed.

Although from the first planning reports about Covent Garden onwards there was general agreement on what the building's new function might be, detailed examination of how its adaptation would be carried out lagged behind the debate on its restoration. Both the first Draft Plan of 1968 and the Revised Plan of 1971 referred to uses broadly similar to those which now fill the building – primarily small specialist shops and eating places.[4] At the time of their publication, when it was envisaged that there would be extensive redevelopment in the area, the retention of the building was felt to have the double virtue of preserving a reminder of Covent Garden's past history and creating a haven to which those disrupted by the changes all around could retreat.[5] In this last respect what has in fact occurred is almost the reverse of early intentions, for the success in re-establishing the market in its new role has partly stemmed from the revival of the whole district following the decision to keep most of its existing buildings. The number of traders in the reopened market who have local origins is really quite small.

The decisions made about the building before the market departed were of course taken with the Plan's proposals for its reuse in mind; in particular the fact that the iron roofs were to be kept could be seen as a triumph for the claims of use or amenity against the claims of restoration. But no more than general resolutions could be debated till its fabric could be thoroughly investigated, which could not happen till the market was out and the first restoration contract under way. Though it was said at the time that the start of work on the project would not 'close any options regarding the detailed use of the building' the stripping away of some of the later additions, notably the offices on the east terrace, did immediately affect the amount of letting space available.[6] Without the peculiar circumstance of having to learn about the building as the job progressed all kinds of matters might have been settled far earlier.

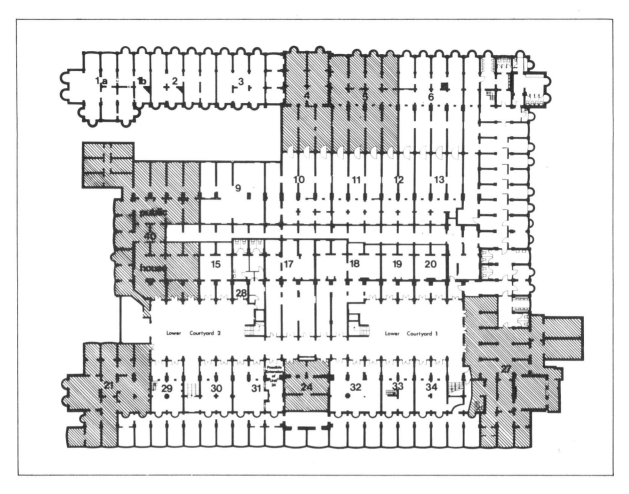

If as work started events seemed to be running ahead of themselves two decisions made in Winter 1974–5 determined more closely than before how the building would function. The first, already discussed, concerned the opening up of the two lower courtyards: once that was settled the main components of the plan as it now is were fixed (Figures 55–56). The second involved the rooms on the first floor of the four ranges. Amongst the first suggestions for these rooms was the proposal that those in the two outer ranges should be turned into twelve flats (eight for two people, four for one person each) while those in the two ranges flanking Central Avenue, which were rather poorly lit because of the iron roofs, could become studio units. The enthusiasm for getting housing into at least part of the building derived from a wider policy of trying to increase the residential population of the area but in this instance, however sympathetic everyone might be to the general aim, there were at least two snags. In the eyes of the GLC Director of Housing all the flats envisaged were far too cramped and too close to the noise and activity of the public areas below: 'extreme difficulty could be encountered in selecting the correct type of tenant for this unusual accommodation'. Even if twenty people could be found who were willing to put up with the disadvantages for the sake of being so close to the heart of things (twenty deaf insomniacs?), converting the first floor

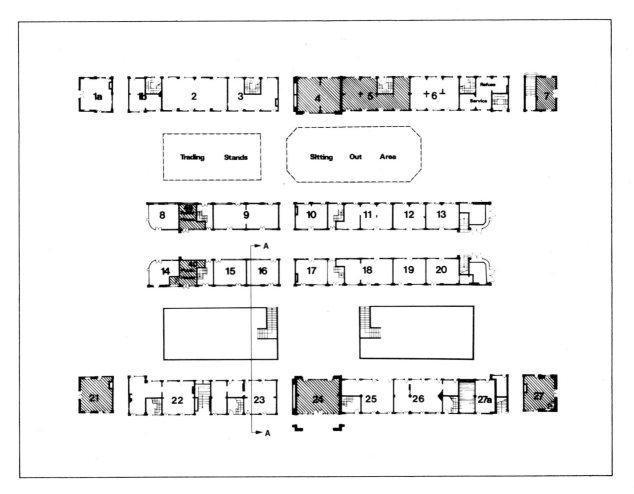

56
Ground floor letting plan (line A A indicates the section which is part of Fig 42).

rooms into flats would have cost about £5,000 a unit more than providing the same kind of housing elsewhere. Confronted with the reluctance of other branches of the Council to support the scheme the Covent Garden Committee was forced to change tracks and put offices where they had hoped housing might go (Figure 57).[7]

With the matter of the basements and the first floor settled detailed attention to questions of reuse went into abeyance, or was subsumed in the broader discussions about controlling the costs of the entire project. But once the final contract was under way the need to establish how exactly each space would be filled, and how the tenants would be chosen, became much more urgent. It was one thing to speak generally of shops and restaurants, quite another to determine what mixture and distribution of such uses would best ensure the building's success.

The first analysis of these problems, made in November 1977, laid down the essential principles which have since been followed. In keeping with the earlier decision that the market should not be let to one overall occupier it recommended against selecting all the tenants according to one theme – say antiques, household goods, or (as in the main Faneuil Hall Marketplace building) food of all kinds. Though cities thrive by nurturing concentrations of special activities it is risky to try and establish a new one instantaneously: far better to introduce a variety of

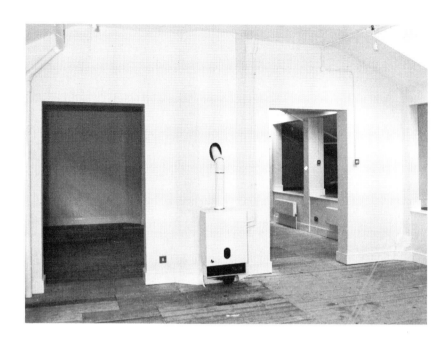

57
Studio interior in the north range.

traders so that if by chance one or two prove unpopular the others may still flourish. Yet while abandoning a total theme it was felt that it would be useful to group some tenants together so that they could benefit each other or help direct the flow of people through the building. In practice, no particularly ambitious clusters have been achieved. Such as they are they have been largely shaped by the complicated layout of the building. The sale of food (for instance Peelers Restaurant and shops dealing in groceries, sweets, tea and coffee) is concentrated in the north range because of its access to space where people can sit out; clothing shops are strung along the south side of Central Avenue partly in the hope that by trading at two levels–ground and basement–they will help lure customers to the lower courtyards; and the units in the courtyards have been leased to the most specialist shops of all, the kind that people are happy to search out and linger over.

There were two other suggestions in the first full report on the letting of the building. One was that it could not hope to flourish on a convenience or passing trade but had to establish itself in the public imagination as somewhere of a quite distinct nature, a place with a reputation throughout London and further afield. So secondly, to ensure that the kind of shops needed to complete this ambition were secured it was recommended that the Council should seek the advice of commercial marketing consultants. To that end, the firm of Donaldsons were appointed early in 1978 to help decide on the tenant mix and management methods, and subsequently to act as joint letting agents.[8]

The Selection of Tenants

The concern to obtain the right combination of tenants occurs in the establishment of any kind of shopping centre, whether it be a new development with two or three key traders ('anchor tenants' as they are called) or one such as at Covent Garden with a more evenly balanced mixture. In order to achieve the best selection it is customary to avoid the straightforward practice of offering space to the highest bidder in favour of the system of agreement by negotiation. With such a system it is easier to discriminate forcefully in the choice of tenants and, if needs be, to search out retailers of the kind needed to fulfill the overall plan. The special circumstances of this case – notably the desire to respect the building and the need for the Council to be as fair as possible to all applicants – made the use of agreement by negotiation particularly appealing. The method adopted involved at least four stages. Once the initial applications had been received, the existing shops and restaurants (of those that had them) were visited anonymously by the staff of Donaldsons or the Planning Team to make a preliminary assessment of how suitable they might be – an exhausting and indigestion-inducing campaign of consumer inspection. There followed interviews which helped appraise how competent and committed the applicants were, and how sympathetic they might be to the special character of the building. From the inspections and interviews a first short-list was made for the Covent Garden Committee to examine. Finally, when negotiations with selected applicants had helped whittle the list down still further, the leasing of each unit was sanctioned by the Chairman and Minority Leader of the Committee. The odd man out in this process was the pub at the west end of Central Avenue, where because of the amount of interest shown by brewers and caterers of apparently equal suitability the more conventional system of inviting offers was reverted to.

Described in an abstract way the selection of tenants, though perhaps a bit over-diligent, sounds fairly straightforward. In reality it was far from simple, partly because of the number of stages involved (which must have seemed to many like a bureaucratic labyrinth), and even more because of the number of applicants dealt with. In the reopened building there are thirty-five retail or catering units, plus the pub and the restaurant which it is intended should occupy greenhouses re-erected on the east terrace. By May 1979 there had been over 800 applicants for these spaces. Though of course many dropped out for one reason or another, and many were manifestly unsuitable, the number from this huge entry that made their way through to the stage of serious negotiations was large: the first selected list of retailers contained sixty-eight names, and of caterers twenty-three names.[9] Because of the number of people showing interest, the aim of filling the building to a pre-conceived plan has been largely achieved, with no need to retreat into the nether world of jeans and hamburgers. Coincidentally another aim has been accomplished, that of starting out with traders of known quality. In the world of retail marketing as elsewhere, it is always easier to start with a high reputation and slip slightly lower than to start at the bottom and work up. Yet the mixture of applicants contained some surprises which led to modification in the original letting outline. Coin and stamp dealers showed less interest in taking space in the building than might have been expected given their traditional association with the area. A good number of booksellers were keen to move in, but eventually far fewer did so than were planned for. Some trades which were not included at all in the outline scheme applied in quite high numbers, for instance hairdressers and opticians, and clothes shops showed such enthusiasm that they now occupy slightly more space in the market than first intended.

Agreement to lease signed with the tenants finally chosen enabled them to start work on shop-fitting (Figures 58–59). Each unit was little more than a bare shell with services laid in, though of course all had their shop-fronts already installed. Some units are so small that fitting them out was bound to be fairly simple but the pub and the restaurants had to somehow squeeze in their equipment and tortuous ventilation apparatus.[10] Tenants have been allowed to choose their shopfront colours, in con-consultation with the Council, and to select their fascia lettering from a set of standard patterns, though in Central Avenue they have had less freedom because the shopfronts were handed over already painted in their handsome brown and cream liveries, and the lettering there has been limited to a distinctive type cut in wood following the style of examples already existing.

As the units were completed the final leases were signed: for shops, fifteen year leases with three year reviews, and for restaurants twenty-five year leases with five year reviews. In addition there is a charge to help cover management and servicing, both of them expensive items in a building such as this whose layout makes it hard to look after. Deliveries cannot be made directly to the shops but have to be brought by trolley from two loading bays: in turn, refuse has to be carted to a mysterious room in the north range where it is compacted into solid cubes before being taken away. Because it is intended that the shops will stay open late (until 8 pm) the hours that the building has to be supervised and cleaned are long, and because it cannot be closed up at night it has to be under a round the clock watch. The work of caring for the market is entrusted to a manager and two deputies appointed by the Council.

The final aspect of retailing is the reuse of some of the cast iron stands from the Flower Market in the open space at the west end of the north hall (Figure 60).[11] Here forty of the stands have been re-erected to be let on weekly or monthly terms to craftsmen and traders who want to be in the building but have not been given (or have not wanted) permanent space. The idea of having a slightly more casual trade such as this helps preserve, in polite guise, some of the animation which used to fill the place.

In judging the success of the building's reuse everyone will have their own opinions. Where the restoration is concerned the layman may be daunted by esoteric talk about the Building Acts and structural defects but anyone who shops can voice an opinion on the way it has been filled. Some finding it too smart and new will recall nostalgically the grubby chaos of the old market, others will acclaim it in terms which make it sound like the new Elysium, and between the two extremes will probably be thousands who enjoy their visit but take home with them some grumble or other–perhaps about the choice of shops, the lack of parking or the character of other visitors. From a mixture of such reactions will come a reputation of success or failure. This though is not hypermarket or a department store where retail profits are the final measure of achievement. It matters as much that through using the building people grow to admire it for its great architectural qualities; that after all is why it has been preserved. If Fowler's design, and the lessons that stem from it, are duly recognised the success will be complete.

58 (facing page, top)
Design by Garnett, Cloughley Blakemore and Associates for the basement of Peelers Restaurant.

59 (facing page, bottom)
Design proposal by John Michael Design Consultants for Kickers Shoes in Central Avenue.

60
Artist's impression of a stand from the Flower Market as re-erected in the north hall.

The Flower Market

Of the other market buildings around the Piazza, one had its fortunes completely transformed as a result of the Minister's decision following the 1971 Covent Garden Public Inquiry. The intention of the first plan for the area was that the Flower Market should be demolished to make way for an international conference centre, a facility that was felt to be very much needed in Central London. Following the announcement in 1973 that the building had been listed, and a subsequent change of heart about the conference centre idea, the Flower Market won a full reprieve.[12] Having been saved it presented some of the same problems of restoration and reuse as Fowler's building had done.

In some ways the case of the Flower Market was simpler. Although constructed in three stages its layout was not nearly as complicated as that of the earlier building. Its four main parts – the main hall, the low building on its west side known as the covered way, the Edwardian addition on its northeast corner and its basement – were all clearly distinguished, and none seemed to pose a problem to compare with the 'roofs on-roofs off' controversy over the later additions to Fowler's work. As its different parts were distinct so the question of dividing the building up was less contentious. And since it was planned that the restoration and conversion should be done by the tenant to whom the building was leased the debate about its future was not protracted but concentrated on the choice of a sympathetic and competent user.

The process of selecting a tenant started with newspaper advertisements in Summer 1975 inviting suggestions about how the building might be used. To these came literally a hundred and one replies, of which the most highly developed and promising were four proposals: an exhibition centre, a theatre project, a tropical garden (a GLC Parks Department idea) and a museum for London Transport. All sounded appealing – what, for instance, would have been nicer than to find an exotic indoor garden in the heart of London? – but it was the London Transport submission that was finally chosen as most appropriate to the building. Their collection of road vehicles, railway carriages and engines, models and other objects connected with the history of transport in London was at that time exhibited at Syon Park in West London: the move to a more central site promised the likelihood of more visits and the chance to arrange the collection in a more systematic way. The agreement to lease the main hall of the Flower Market to the museum, and later also the covered way, was made in 1977: London Transport was to carry out the restoration, with advice from the Historic Buildings Division, and to adapt the building to its new use.[13]

Since cast and wrought iron were more fully exploited in the construction of the Flower Market than in Fowler's market the problems of its restoration focused mainly on those materials. Surprisingly, although the building was put up at about the same time and by the same firm of contractors as the iron roofs added to its neighbour, its ironwork showed more signs of wear than that on the other building. More of its roof members needed attention – they were mostly bound up using the same method described earlier – and the large semi-circular windows at the end of its two main naves were found to have bowed outwards, cracking their enclosing arches: the ironwork of each window had to be carefully cleaned, and the rust raked out of its joints, before being bolted together again to remove the distortion.[14] Cleaning the old paint off the ironwork was more troublesome than in previous experience because of the need to use wet rather than dry grit-blasting after the danger of lead poisoning from the work became apparent. But once the ironwork had been cleaned and repaired, the roofs largely reglazed and their leadwork renewed, the major part of the restoration was complete. Thankfully, because the building was to be in single occupation with ample means for escape in the event of fire, no requirement was imposed that the columns be covered with intumescent mastic or any other such material.

Although the Flower Market has never done duty as a bus garage or railway station its layout and character are perfectly fitted for its new role. Not only is it of the right date and design to complement many of the objects on show but its space and height enable them to be got into place quite easily and to be properly appreciated once they are there (Figures 61–62). The only significant alterations needed have been the infilling of the short arm towards Wellington Street in order to house the coffee shop, offices and toilets, and the construction of two raised platforms (the larger of which has supports running through the basement to the ground beneath) to exhibit some of the trams and railway vehicles. In other respects the display installed fits the shape of the building, with a narrative history of transport in London told with the aid of pictures, slides and models around the walls and the larger objects grouped at the centre of the hall and in the covered way. The only foreseeable problem with this arrangement – one similar to that which besets almost every transport museum – is that the thousands coming in from

61 *(right)*
Artist's impression of the interior of the Flower Market converted for use as the London Transport Museum.

62 *(below)*
A West Ham Corporation tramcar (left) and a London County Council tramcar (right) being put into position in the museum.

the Piazza will be so dazzled by the collection of buses, trams, trolley buses and railway engines that the wall displays will get overlooked: but there is more chance, now the museum is in such a good location, that people will make enough repeated visits to get beyond the most stunning objects and heed the other material on display.

An American Contrast.
The Faneuil Hall Marketplace, Boston

A restoration once done is unlikely to be repeated, however much those involved might appreciate the chance to improve on their first experience. Because each project is unique it is difficult to conceive what the results might have been if it had been tackled in a different way; or if the alternatives can be imagined, their merits may not be admitted. Any account of a particular project such as the GLC restoration work at Covent Garden may end up sounding like a eulogy simply because it has no comparative context. Though there is no precise remedy to such parochialism, because there have been no exactly similar projects, it may be possible to a broader view by setting the work at Covent Garden alongside the restoration of the Faneuil Hall Marketplace in Boston (Figures 63–64).

To any trans-Atlantic traveller both projects may seem like echoes of each other, not just because the two restorations were undertaken almost simultaneously (the American slightly ahead of the English one) but because the buildings are so similar in style and date. The decision to build a new market in Boston followed the incorporation of the city in 1822 and the site chosen was mainly infilled land immediately behind the famous Faneuil Hall. On this were to be laid out three buildings: a market hall, which came to be known as the Quincy Market after Mayor Josiah Quincy who initiated the scheme, and two flanking rows of commercial buildings along North and South Market Streets. Construction of the central building was a civic responsibility but the sites of the other two were sold to a series of developers on condition that they erect buildings to the design of the architect to the whole project. The market hall opened in 1826 with 128 stalls serving both retail and wholesale trade on its ground floor, and a large exhibition hall above.[15]

The genesis of the Boston scheme was therefore very different to the aristocratic origins of Fowler's building, closer in fact to the market projects in English provincial towns. It was also on a far larger scale: three buildings instead of one, all over five hundred feet long. Yet they have in common that both Fowler and Alexander Parris, the architect of the Faneuil Hall Markets, chose to work in the Greek Revival style and both realised the suitability of granite to this type of building. Parris not only built granite porticoes on both ends of the Quincy Market but used the same material in a trabeated system for the construction of the other main facades, an innovation which brought economy in building and allowed for wider window openings.[16] Having been completed within four years of each other the works of Fowler and Parris both went through the same cycle of adulation and criticism, suffered in the same way from additions and alterations, and finally became redundant with the relocation of the function that had been their mainstay.

When the question of their future was raised in the 1960s Faneuil Hall Markets had the advantage (like Covent Garden) of being in a conspicuous location, placed between the waterfront and the Government Centre, where a new City Hall was about to be completed. They were also to benefit from the growing preoccupation in America with the declining reputation and prosperity of downtown areas which suburban residents felt no desire or necessity to visit. This and other concerns, not all of them to do with the architectural merits of the buildings, meant that the preservation campaign in Boston was wide in scope, so wide in fact that newspaper descriptions of it brim over with the names of politicians, voluntary organisations, architects and entrepreneurs.[17] Sorting through such accounts what stands out is the crucial part played by the commercial developer who took the lease on the buildings and converted them, and his dependence on the local banking community; neither of them matters which would astonish an American, or anyone familiar with the building of new shopping centres in Britain, but quite a far cry from the continuity of municipal control exercised at Covent Garden.

The work at Faneuil Hall Markets started in 1968 with the submission of a five-volume report on the buildings to the Boston Redevelopment Authority, prepared by the Society for New England Antiquities and Architectural Heritage Inc. This impressive document, which included a meticulous account of their history as well as an architectural and financial appraisal of their restoration potential, helped convince the city authorities of the project's viability and assisted in obtaining federal funding for its first stage. Begun in 1972, this involved the renovation of exteriors, especially the removal of the jumble of roof additions which had been made to the North and South Markets from the 1860s onwards: had the conditions of these been better a case might been made for the retention of some of them.[18] Meanwhile the selection of a developer to take on the buildings was making topsy-turvy progress, the first firm chosen being later rejected because of its failure to ger financial backing. The choice which finally went through, and got the bankers' support, was of the Rouse Company, best-known at the time of its application as the developer of twenty suburban shopping centres and of the new town called Columbia in Maryland. To secure its commitment, and the redirection of its policy towards a city centre property, was a notable coup. Rouse was designated in 1973 and signed a ninety-nine year lease in 1975. The restored Quincy Market was reopened in 1976 followed in the next two years by the North and South Markets.

The initiative to involve the Rouse Company came from the architect Benjamin Thompson, who having been associated with the earlier, unsucessful application was determined not to let the project perish. His success in winning the interest of Rouse, and subsequently in carrying through the rest of the work as the company's architect, was based on his firm appreciation of how the market buildings could be used as shops and eating places, and how attractive they might be. He and Rouse took as their starting point the buildings' commercial potential, and in keeping with that priority Thompson adopted an approach to their restoration markedly different to that of the architects who worked on the Covent Garden project. He stressed the importance of 'valid continuity – the joining of successive styles in elegant and compatible ways'. Implied in

63 *(facing page, top)*
Faneuil Hall Marketplace, Boston.
Faneuil Hall itself is in the foreground.

64 *(facing page, bottom)*
Faneuil Hall Marketplace, view between
Quincy Market and the North Market
with City Hall (1968) in the background.

this belief was a reluctance to 'restore back' the buildings by reproducing past features which had been destroyed–an approach always associated in America with the restoration of Colonial Williamsburg–and equally a willingness to see new additions made so long as the new work was properly differentiated from the old; in Thompson's words, 'We should not attempt to freeze history but rather strive to enhance its flow'.[19] What this meant in practice was that in the adaptation of the Faneuil Hall Markets to their new use several changes were made to their appearance all of which, in keeping woth Thompson's opinion, can be clearly distinguished. Amongst them are three which are most often remarked on. Along the sides of the Quincy Market building steel and glass canopies have been erected to protect pavement diners and push-cart salesmen–an extension of the retail area of the building similar in intent (though far more obtrusive) to the formation of the lower court-yards at Covent Garden.[20] Inside the same building an opening has been created in the first floor beneath the dome so that people using the ground floor arcade can have the pleasure of looking up into the dome's interior, an advantage gained at the expense of destroying the integrity of the first floor space. And in all the buildings the windows have been filled with single panes of glass rather than the original pattern of smaller panes divided by glazing bars. Since modern designs and materials have been used in all these changes their cumulative effect is to make the fact of the building's reuse absolutely explicit, weakening the impact of the original design. Had the same enthusiasm for yoking new work with old been shown at Covent Garden (where the claims for such an approach were certainly not unheard) the project there would probably have taken a much different direction.

Faneuil Hall Marketplace has been an outstanding public success, with a reported twelve million visitors a year and a retail turnover in 1978 of $54 million.[21] It has come to be regarded as a model of how a speciality centre can assist in the revival of a city's downtown. The reopened Covent Garden has not been in action long enough yet for a comparable assessment to be made of its commercial strength but it is not too early to recognise the different procedures and emphasises of the two projects; above all, contrasts in the way they have been controlled and financed, and in their architectural approach. Starting with buildings remarkably alike, and similar ambitions for their reuse, the two end results are significantly different. Those fortunate to have a chance of visiting the two restorations will enjoy speculating on what might have happened if the methods of both schemes had been transposed.

Chapter 5

The Building in its Setting

The story of Fowler's building illustrates in microcosm one of the most interesting themes in London's history. It has often been assumed that until this century the development of London was essentially unplanned, that it had grown in a haphazard way without any directing authority. True, there was Nash's Regent Street and its less elegant Victorian imitators such as Shaftesbury Avenue and Queen Victoria Street but these barely touched the scale of Haussmann's Paris or the ruthless gridiron plans of American cities. Grand schemes (the argument continues) such as Wren's for rebuilding the City after the Great Fire remained dreams on paper, halted at the outset by the possessiveness of property owners or the absence of an imaginative municipal government capable of seeing them executed. Not till the costs of uncontrolled growth in terms of disease, inconvenience and visual chaos were understood did the idea of planning get a toehold.

The delight to be had in walking through parts of Covent Garden to-day would seem at first to support this thesis. There is nothing grandiose or predictable about the approach from the west along New Row, and the streets and alleys which bisect the area have an intricacy typical of districts which are reputed to have grown pragmatically. Anyone whose preconception of urban planning is a pencil-straight boulevard will be disappointed. Yet much of Covent Garden was in fact planned from the very beginning. In the first sense of the term there was the plan drawn up by the fourth Earl of Bedford and Inigo Jones in the 1630s for the Piazza and the surrounding streets, followed later in the century by Thomas Neale's layout for Seven Dials. Both of these classic plans were of course private rather than civic projects but their intention was essentially the same as a local authority or New Town scheme to-day: like their twentieth-century successors they hoped to realise social as well as physical planning ideals. Even in parts of Covent Garden which show less evidence of self-conscious design there is little reason to think that their initial development was a complete free-for-all.

The involvement of ground landlords as supervising powers did not cease with the completion of the first layout, for the leasehold system under which most of London was built established their continuing interest in their estates. With an eye to maintaining the reversionary value that their properties would have for themselves and their successors they were called on to plan in the second sense, to try and anticipate or adapt to the long term changes affecting the city.

The apparatus and powers of urban landlords like the Bedford family in the southern part of Covent Garden or the Mercers Company in the blocks to the North of Long Acre might well be envied by to-day's town planners. In the first instance it was their decision whether and how to develop their property and what limitations of design or use to place on their leaseholders. At the second stage, as leases began to fall in (anything between twenty-one and ninety-nine years later, depending on the time and place) they were free to rethink their policies in the light of changed circumstances: to relet to the existing tenant or to grant a fresh building lease for a more up-to-date scheme. Through convenants or agreements attached to leases it was possible to dictate the design of buildings, how they should be maintained and what use they could be put to. Continuity of control over the estate, exercised for the family by a team of agents, surveyors and lawyers, was just as important as the making of a spectacular first plan.[1]

Though he would not have answered to the title of planner that essentially was the part played by an official like J R Bourne, steward to the ninth Duke of Bedford. Cross-examined by a parliamentary committee in 1887 he made clear his conviction that the powers he wielded contributed just as much to the public welfare as to the Duke's private interests: 'Speaking broadly, and socially, for the general community, the existence of these large estates, well laid out, and well cared for, and well looked after, because they have got one united freeholder, the freeholder of the entire area, is, in a manner of speaking, the salvation of London'.[2] At the same time he was willing to admit as proof of landowners' responsiveness to outside forces that their powers were not absolute: they could not command anyone to build on their estate, or to take up residence, nor could they prevent a tenant from leaving to live or set up business elsewhere. 'Any attempt', he insisted, 'to impose an unusual term, either as to the amount of rent or restrictive conditions, or outlay by the tenant, or anything of that class, would simply result in having the property empty; no one would take it'.[3] His reference to the vulnerability of his work to forces beyond his influence will sound familiar to any brow-beaten contemporary planner.

In theory it was open to a ground landlord and his staff to completely transform an estate as leases fell in but seldom was such a radical step contemplated, either because not enough leases reverted to the owner simultaneously to make extensive replanning possible or because buildings on the estate did not wear out in unison. The more usual story was of gradual renewal within the original layout, carried out by existing tenants in return for new leases. Unadventurous though this may sound it was a sensible way of allowing change to take place without adopting a new-fangled scheme which might prove unworkable. So in Covent Garden the Bedfords watched over the area's transformation from a residential to a primarily commercial district. To ease this change they encouraged piecemeal rebuilding and alterations, with the result that what is seen to-day are largely nineteenth-century buildings within the seventeenth-century street plan. The policies of building renewal followed by them (and their equivalents elsewhere in London) were in no respect startling but they proved to be financially sound and they left a most agreeable visual legacy.

Seen in the context of a general estate policy of the kind just described the construction of the market building can be regarded as a classic example of the accommodation of change within an existing framework, conceding to a commercial development which had far outgrown first expectation. It remains in this final chapter to outline some of the other continuities in the history of building in the area.

Victorian Improvements

The process of renewing buildings in Covent Garden, or at least refronting them, started within decades of the first development so that buildings which appear to be original may in fact be of the second or third generation on their site. The chance to renew most often occurred at the end of a lease or when something untoward happened. For instance, Nos 5–8 Henrietta Street were rebuilt after two of the four houses collapsed in 1730: Nos 7 and 8 still have internal features of that date concealed behind their nineteenth century fronts. Opposite, most of the north side of the street (where St Peter's Hospital and its neighbours now stand) was rebuilt a year or so earlier to common specifications, 'so that the whole Range of new Houses . . . may appear Regularly uniformly and handsomely built'.[4] In King Street at least two houses on the south side were completely renewed in the 1670s when they were only about forty years old. On the north side, No 27 was reconstructed in 1690–1 with a projecting shopfront, a sign of the way in which retailing was reaching into the area: it had to be replaced yet again after a fire in 1759 and was given its present handsome appearance in the following century after being taken over by the Westminster Fire Office. At the Piazza end of King Street the building of No 43 in 1716–17 involved the demolition of the westernmost bays of Jones's arcaded buildings. The grand Baroque mansion which took their place (the last building in the Piazza area to be lived in by a titled person) has survived an extraordinary versatile existence with most of its fabric intact: at various times it has housed a hotel, the headquarters of the Royal Institute of British Architects, a music hall (in a large addition at the rear), three clubs and the offices and store of a major market trader (Figure 65).[5]

The completion of No 43 King Street, set down so stridently alongside the Piazza ranges, marked the first steps in the break-up of the architectural cohesion of the central layout. Further sections were lost later in the eighteenth century. When in 1670 part of the row at the southeast corner of the Piazza collapsed there was no doubt about its being reinstated in the original style, but when in 1769 the same row was gutted by fire its replacement was remarkably different. Instead of having an arcaded walkway the brick-fronted houses were set back behind railings, each with a rusticated doorcase surmounted by a triangular pediment, as if part of a Bloomsbury Square had lost itself further south (Figure 66). Later, the house on the west corner of the Piazza and James Street was rebuilt above arcade level in a bald and inappropriate way.[6]

By the opening of the nineteenth century few of the original 1630s buildings survived in an untouched state but no radical overall changes had been made. The Bedford policy of gradual renewal on existing sites continued during the Victorian period – 'Georgian London persisted in spirit as well as body', as Donald Olsen remarks – but opinion on the merits of such a cautious approach had begun to divide along strikingly familiar lines.[7] Those who hankered after a more comprehensive programme of improvement were bound to be disappointed by such faltering progress, and to blame it on aristocratic lack of vision bolstered by the customs attached to the leasehold system. Alongside growing criticism of the way the Bedfords managed the market ran the complaint that despite their extensive powers they were failing to allow for its growth. As the *Builder* put it in 1878: 'In any other country but England, and in far less important cities than London, a municipality would have taken care to see that such a square as Covent-garden was enlarged when the time came for rebuilding the houses enclosing it'. But if the Bedfords

65
*43 King Street, a photograph taken in
1973 when the building was still in use
for market trading. As much as
possible of its original entrance (with a
recessed porch behind a pair of Corinthian
columns) has recently been reinstated.*

66
*The north and east sides of the Piazza
after the rebuilding of Little Piazza
in 1769.*

67
*Bedford Chambers, a photograph taken
in 1921. In the background is the
Tavistock Hotel, built 1860–8.*

were passing over a chance to give the market more room – so inviting outside intervention – it was not simply because of blinkered conservatism. By the time the need for the enlargement of the market was apparent the historical importance of the Piazza area was more deeply appreciated, so placing a further inhibition on large-scale remodelling. The ninth Duke was told by his steward in 1873, 'I am not without misgivings that the destruction of any portion of this distinctive feature in Covent Garden Architecture will produce a considerable amount of unfavourable public criticism'. The Duke was under no compulsion to recognise such criticism – other property owners of the time seem not to have allowed the destruction of comparable historic buildings to test their consciences – but it gave a foretaste of the way in which replanning might be limited in the future.[8]

The steward's warning and the *Builder* criticism were both occasioned by the proposal to rebuild the part of the Piazza ranges that lay between James Street and No 43 King Street. The worry that this project engendered was heightened by the fact that this was virtually the last section of the original design to survive: the range east of James Street had in part been destroyed to make way for the Floral Hall and in part rebuilt as the Tavistock Hotel. Henry Clutton, who was chosen as architect, decided not to make an exact replica of Jones's work but to repeat its most characteristic features on an enlarged scale. Behind its uniform facade Bedford Chambers (as the new building was called) accommodated a hotel, residential flats (then an innovation), shops and a warehouse (Figure 67). The same *Builder* critic found such cramming of different uses behind a single exterior 'not a wise or logical mode of building houses which are to stand in their places for at least a century' and might therefore have been surprised – could he have known it – to see Clutton's building flourishing when other more blatantly functional works have passed away.

Bedford Chambers was the most distinguished of a number of designs which Clutton made (or supervised) for the rebuilding of properties in the area, some of them a trifle dull but all sympathetic to their setting. He designed No 41–2 King Street for one of the leaseholders displaced by his work in the Piazza. No 1–4 opposite followed in 1883–5 and its twin on the other side of the church, No 34 Henrietta Street, a few years later. On the south and east sides of the Piazza his influence can be seen in the building, once a hotel but now a bank, at the corner of Southampton and Henrietta Streets and Russell Chambers alongside the Flower Market. All of these buildings play on the same French Renaissance theme with Portland stone ground storey and red brick elevation above, the architraves, string courses and balustrade being also in stone.

Moving beyond the Piazza, the nineteenth-century rebuildings on old sites are too numerous to describe in detail. Together they provide a catalogue of fluctuating stylistic enthusiasms, from Charles Gray's Italianate No 22 Henrietta Street (1857–8), via J M Brydon's St Peter's Hospital in the red brick Queen Anne style (1881–2) to Lutyens's first venture in the 'Wrenaissance' manner, the 'Country Life' Building in Tavistock Street (1904–5, now renamed 'Hudson House' after the magazine's first editor). Though these and others were all built to a generous scale – the Lutyens block with its colossal chimneys rises well above its neighbours – none were too flagrantly disruptive to their surroundings.

However, it would be quite wrong to suggest that the Covent Garden area passed through the Victorian period with only moderate adjustments to its appearance. Its location at the centre of a city exploding in size and population, plus the work it offered, created the two most typical problems of the time: the wish to improve communications, both to service its own wants and to help the rest of London, and the need to tackle the patches of slum housing which existed within and around its boundaries. For those who were prepared to overlook, as many were, the question of what became of those displaced, there appeared to be a single cure to both headaches: to break a new road through the worst streets and courts, improving them by wiping them off the map. Only as an afterthought was it appreciated that one effect of carving through a built-up district was to exacerbate the problems of surrounding streets as those evicted shifted to the nearest possible surviving housing. In Covent Garden, where the odd hours and irregularity of so many jobs forced thousands to live near their work, the impact of such disruption was especially painful.[9]

Since the Piazza was designed to be a superior residential enclave the streets enclosing it were quite unsuited to housing the traffic generated by a vigorous market. So the first street improvements designed to penetrate the area (as distinct from those that skirted it, like New Oxford Street and Nash's West Strand improvements) were intended first and foremost to give better access to the market. To the south, the full benefits of the opening of Waterloo Bridge in 1817 could not be felt until a direct link across the Strand was made. The creation of Wellington Street (the southern half of the street so named to-day) was carried out by the Commissioners of Woods and Forests in 1833–5: the English Opera House, which had stood in its way, had conveniently burnt down and was subsequently rebuilt beside the new street. At the same time the Commissioners opened up the north end of Bow Street, where the elegant 'Kemble's Head' pub stands, thereby creating a through route to Long Acre: this in turn was extended by the making of Endell Street a decade later as part of the campaign to eradicate the St Giles rookery.[10]

A further scheme considered by the Commissioners was at first less fruitful despite the fact that it had the support of the seventh Duke of Bedford. The intention was to form a new approach from the west by extending Cranbourn Street to a junction with King Street, including a link to Floral Street 'for the purpose of removing some objectionable courts, of improving a very inferior locality'. The Duke offered to subsidize the Commissioners' project but neither they nor the local parish felt able to carry it out. It therefore became the first major street improvement executed by the Metropolitan Board of Works after its establishment in 1855. The Bedford Estate finally contributed £15,000 and paid the entire cost of the branch to Floral Street.[11] Garrick Street, as it was called, was completed in 1861 and was lined not with new housing for those who had been displaced, but with the kind of new uses thought fitting for such a thoroughfare: Debenham, Storr and Sons' auction rooms at the King Street corner (1860, Arthur Allom), the dextrous gothic building designed by Arthur Blomfield for Heaton, Butler and

68

The making of Garrick Street, a watercolour by T H Shepherd showing clearance in progress for its intended junction with St Martin's Lane.

Baynes' stained glass works (1864), and the Garrick Club (1864, Frederick Marrable) looking for all it is worth like a bit of Pall Mall which has strayed east (Figure 68).[12]

For those who lost their homes in the Garrick Street improvement the nearest retreat was just to the south in Bedfordbury, described by Sala as 'a devious, slimey little reptile of a place' whose tenements had barely a single window intact. Here by the early 1870s lived over 2,000 people, many of them market workers, in conditions which so alarmed the local Medical Officer of Health that he called on the MBW to clear the area. The scheme agreed to was not quite as far-reaching as he had hoped but seventy-two houses in the courts and alleys on the east side of Bedfordbury were demolished in 1880: 797 slum dwellers were displaced and room was provided for almost that number (though seldom the very same people) in the blocks put up by the Peabody Trust on the site.[13]

Coinciding with the Bedfordbury project ran a campaign to clear the equally infamous courts on the east side of Covent Garden, between Drury Lane and Great Wild Street. Here again the Peabody Trust was called in to fulfill the MBW's obligation to rehouse as many as were made homeless by the demolitions: in this case their four blocks were designed to house 1,620 people.[14] But this did not in one sweep rid Drury Lane of its degenerate reputation for it left untouched the courts to the west of the street on either side of the Theatre Royal. (Figure 69). These were

Duke's Court off Drury Lane,
photographed in 1898 prior to its
demolition.

the subject of a special investigation by the Bedford agent in 1884 at the time of the Royal Commission on the Housing of the Working Classes. Of ninety-nine houses visited, most were in a reasonable state of repair (only eighteen were described as 'bad' or 'very bad') and the overall density of about twelve per house was not too out of the ordinary. The best of the residents, living in Crown Court and Broad Court, included 'Market Salesmen, Musicians at the Theatres, Sergeants and Constables in Police, Printers, etc' but at the other extreme, to the south of the theatre, were 'Market Porters, Shoe Menders, Jobbing Tradesmen and Labourers, with Laundresses and Charwomen' plus the faint threat, unless vigilant action was taken, of crime and prostitution.[15] This perhaps was not as black a picture as was feared but it had the very ingredients which made officialdom anxious, most of all the forcing together of quite respectable workers and their families with the casual poor as both pursued the ever-shrinking supply of central London housing. These courts became the favourite stamping ground of philanthropists and churchmen, who established in the area such institutions as the Drury Lane Christian Mission, the Inns of Court Mission (whose building still survives), the 'Cat and Comfort' working-men's club and a Working Girls' Home.[16] The chance to replan this part of Covent Garden did not arise till the 1890s when the falling in of leases coincided with the maturing of the London County Council scheme for making the Aldwych and Kingsway. By agreement between the Duke of Bedford and the Council the two worst patches were replaced by public housing while in Kemble Street, Bruce House–one of the finest early designs of the LCC Architects' Department–was erected as a substitute for the many lodging houses destroyed by the progress of the new streets.[17]

The Spread of the Market

None of the efforts made by the Bedford Estate to accommodate the market, at first in Fowler's building and later in the three other market buildings around the Piazza, could meet the insatiable demand of traders for more space, especially the need for warehousing for goods which could be held over from one day's trading to the next. One of the advantages that stemmed from the Bedfords' ownership of so much of the land around the market was that they felt able, because of their position as landlords, to permit traders to take premises well beyond the Piazza. They therefore avoided strangling the market by attempting to confine it within the boundaries defined in the 1670 charter. The two controls which enabled them to allow its spread without fearing for their income were a power to insert a covenant in the leases of surrounding buildings insisting that tenants pay a toll on their goods as if they were in the chartered market, and a similar power that any trader having a place in the market should pay a toll on all his goods whether handled through a Bedford property or not. The use of such leasehold covenants seems to have started in the early 1860s in the case of a seedsman's warehouse in Floral Street and a potato salesman's premises in Maiden Lane.[18] From that time onwards it is possible to watch market uses seeping into the neighbourhood, at first slowly but gathering pace before and after the First World War.

King Street and Long Acre provide two obvious examples of this process. When John Tallis engraved his perspective view of King Street in 1838–40 there appear to have been only five buildings still totally in domestic use but amongst the rest none carried trades relating to the market. Forty years later five addresses had market business at them, including the seedsmen Barr and Sugden who had built special premises with a conservatory on the roof at Nos 12–13. A further leap to 1920 showed little substantial change but by the outbreak of the Second World War nineteen firms, mostly fruit merchants, had places in the street (Figure 70).[19] Long Acre had been famous since the seventeenth century as the centre of the coach building trade: by 1791 at least twenty-five major firms had premises in the street, along with subsidiary trades such as saddlers, upholsterers and lamp makers (Figure 71). Some made the transition to the automobile age by turning themselves into motor salerooms or repair shops but most gave way directly to the invasion of market users. The changeover, which was remarked on the in 1910s, was virtually complete by 1930 when thirty-six market firms had Long Acre addresses.[20]

From the point of view of a successful business this takeover of the neighbouring streets meant eventually that its tenancy in the main market buildings seemed less essential. For instance, the firm of George Monro

70 (facing page, top)
Traffic congestion in King Street.

71 (facing page, bottom)
Hatchett's coach building works in Long Acre, an engraving of 1783.

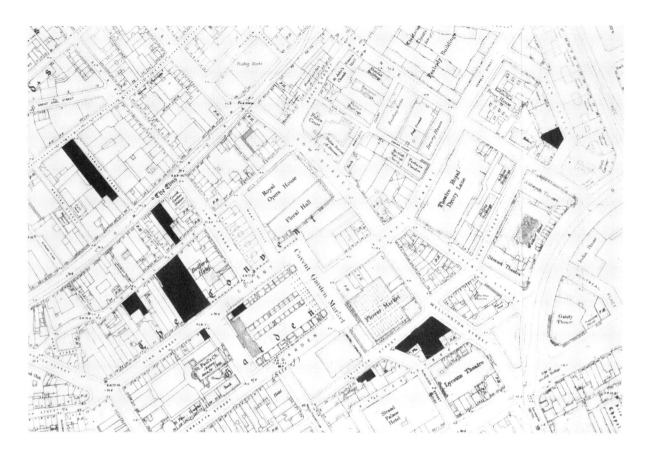

72
The premises of George Monro Ltd in 1935.

Ltd was first established in 1862 with a place in the north range of Fowler's building, dealing in locally grown produce. As they expanded into the flower trade, the import business and horticultural sundries they took up premises in nearly every major street – notably a large warehouse in Langley Street in 1925 and 43 King Street in 1933 – till a map of their locations had to cover almost the whole area (Figure 72).[21] Another prominent firm, T J Poupart Ltd, started through the familiar step of a market gardener edging into the commission business. From a beginning at a warehouse in Drury Lane they took a tenancy in Central Avenue in 1901 before spreading to Bow Street, Shelton Street and most conspicuously to Long Acre, where they took a building lease from the Mercers Company in 1936 to reconstruct Nos 107–15 as their headquarters.[22]

In 1921, only three years after the sale of the Covent Garden Estate by the Bedfords, it was estimated that half the trade in the market was transacted outside the charter area. As to the final extent of its influence, by the early 1960s businesses in some way connected with the market occupied thirty acres, or about fifteen times the space first assigned to its use.[23]

The Market Moves Out

In their position as urban landlords the Bedford family and their officials played a pioneering role, first in the way they developed their Covent

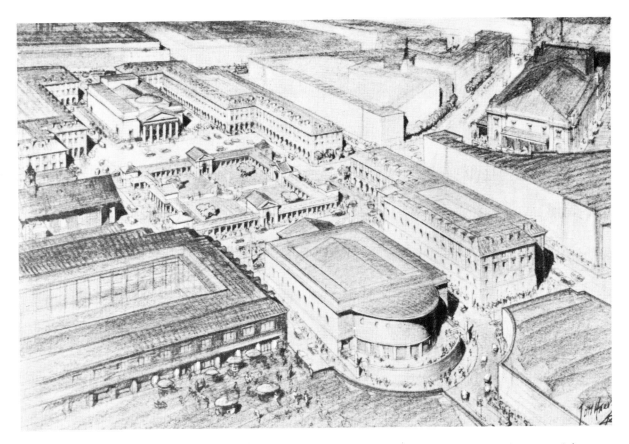

73
The Royal Academy proposal for replanning the Piazza area, 1942.

Garden estate, then in their readiness to allow its commercial transformation and finally in their spectacular decision in 1913 to sell it. Once the transfer to the Covent Garden Estate Company had been completed, and the company in its turn had begun to sell many of the important properties on the estate, the continuity of control that the area had experienced over almost three centuries came to end. Throughout the rather torpid inter-war debate about the future of the market and its possible relocation little reference was made to how the consequences of its moving out would be dealt with. Only during the Second World War, when in response to the devastation brought by bombing the most idealistic dreams began to flourish, did anyone conceive how Covent Garden without its market might look. The scheme proposed in 1942 by a Royal Academy Committee chaired by Sir Edwin Lutyens showed Fowler's building modified to become a public promenade between a new Opera House to the north and a concert hall to the south, but gave no impression how the area beyond the Piazza and its immediate neighbourhood might be treated (Figure 73).[24]

In the lapse of time before the final decision was made that the market should move the apparatus of town planning, set up partly to fulfill wartime hopes, had acquired the powers to control what would happen in the area as a result of this unprecedented change. What in effect had occurred was that local authority planners had taken on much of the role once played by urban landlords, including the authority to decide about land use, densities, and building renewal. If they did not recognise that ancestry in their administrative position they did lay claim to it where their powers of urban design were concerned. The first significant planning report on the future of Covent Garden was self-consciously historical in its ambitions: there was, it said, 'the opportunity of creating in Covent Garden, a new twentieth-century town community, re-capturing the spirit of London's 18th. century squares'.[25] At the same time, perhaps without knowing it, planners inherited some of the anxiety that had beset land-owners like the Bedfords, the fear that however conscientious their estate management might be it could be overtaken by forces beyond their grasp. Now the anxiety was that without an adequate plan the area would be transformed in a way that no-one could wish for: 'In the absence of strategic controls on uses and a compre-hensive plan for the area, an immense rush of redevelopment, piecemeal and uncoordinated, could be expected on the removal of the market'.[26]

Once it was definitely known that the market was to be transferred to Nine Elms a special planning team for the Covent Garden area was appointed by the Greater London Council, the City of Westminster and the Borough of Camden. In 1968 it produced its first Draft Plan which, if not as innovative for its time as Inigo Jones's scheme had been in the 1630s, did at least represent what was then some of the most up-to-date thinking on the treatment of city centre problems, especially the hand-ling of traffic and the relationship between old and new development. Surveys of the area showed that though it was dominated by the market (employing over 5,000 people) it was characterised just as much by its huge variety of other trades and activities, many of them inter-dependent: the Royal Opera House, the Theatre Royal Drury Lane and other theatres supported by costumiers and scenery workshops; publishers linked to printers, engravers and booksellers; specialist shops, craft shops and other one-man business. It was hoped that this quality of mixture and association, which gave the area so much of its vibrance, could be maintained.[27] Turning from work to residence, the team noted that though the population had shrunk considerably (in 1966 it was calculated to be 3,300) it included a high proportion of people with long links in the district and 'an unusually well balanced ratio between manual and non-manual occupations': the existing population was listed first amongst the categories of people likely to be served by the increased housing provision proposed.[28] And where the actual fabric of the area was concerned the planners were again impressed by what they found: not just the well-known monuments like St Paul's Church but the large number of buildings which gave the streets around such visual variety. The best of these were mapped according to 'lines of character' or 'lines of visual structure' where it was intended many of the buildings should be preserved to provide 'links with the past and familiar' in the midst of new development: Fowler's market building, resplendent in its new use, was to be a prominent feature on one such route.[29]

In describing the results of their surveys the planning team made the area sound like everyone's urban ideal—a place of highly varied activity supporting a close-knit, well balanced population. Yet against the claims of its existing character had to be set the opportunites that its redevelop-ment presented for improving its deficiencies (for instance, its lack of open space) and for meeting some of the wider needs of Central London.

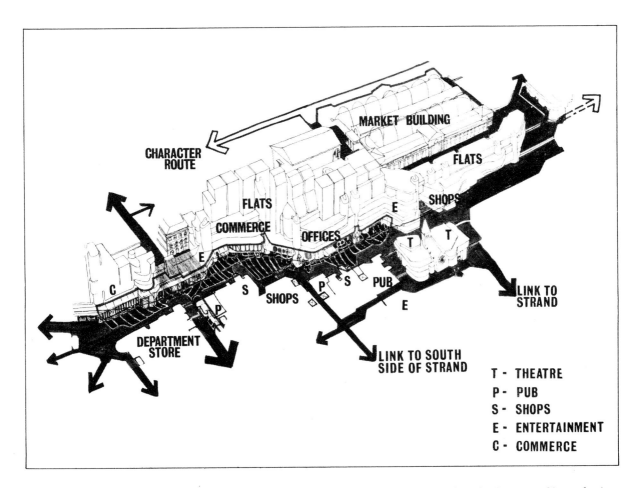

MARKET BUILDING

CHARACTER ROUTE

FLATS

SHOPS

FLATS

COMMERCE

OFFICES

E

C

E

S

SHOPS

P

S

PUB

E

LINK TO STRAND

DEPARTMENT STORE

P

LINK TO SOUTH SIDE OF STRAND

T - THEATRE
P - PUB
S - SHOPS
E - ENTERTAINMENT
C - COMMERCE

74
*One of the drawings illustrating the
1968 Draft Plan.*

As described and illustrated in the Draft Plan the impact of introducing
new facilities and uses would have been dramatic, some would say
devastating (Figure 74). They included a new open space of about four
acres bestriding Long Acre with possibly a sports centre adjoining it,
new hotels, more provision for the arts and entertainment, and the building of a conference centre in the southeast corner of the Piazza. Most
contentious of all, if only because their introduction seemed to have
determined so much else, was the intention of making new roads through
the area. Two new 'spine' routes, sunk below ground level for most of
their path, were to run near to its north and south boundaries, one largely
parallel to Shorts Gardens and the other to the south of Henrietta
Street: they would have been joined at their east and west ends partly by
existing roads and partly by newly constructed ones. Alongside the
southern 'spine', and linked to it, was to be another sunken route, four
lanes wide, to relieve the Strand of its eastbound traffic. The effect of
imposing this new road pattern on the district would have been to
divide it into roughly three areas, with new development to the north
and south leaving a central wedge where there would have been far less
new building. Pedestrians could enjoy a ground level existence in the
central area but in the new parts they were to be given their own raised
walkways, completely segregated from other traffic.[30]

This plan was subsequently revised, allowing more hotel space but less

75
Protest in Covent Garden, 1972.

room for entertainment and the arts, and slightly altering the road proposals.[31] In its modified version it formed the basis of an application to the Department of the Environment for the declaration of a Comprehensive Development Area covering ninety-six acres. This was the subject of a lengthy Public Inquiry in Summer 1971.

The way in which the GLC proposals were received is now part of planning history. Having been formulated according to the accepted wisdom of the time—for instance, the road projects were clearly indebted to the Buchanan Report on *Traffic in Towns*—they were amongst the first and most spectacular victims of the reaction against such grandiose schemes. A hostile press, and a well-organised community association set up to fight the plan at the Public Inquiry, derided what was described as 'an attempt to impose a neat intellectual exercise on to a diverse and uniquely untouched part of a city' (Figure 75).[32] What the planning team appeared to be doing, as the Bedfords in their time never had, was to force the pace of change in a manner insensitive to the physical and social character of the district, defending the need to do so with arguments which when applied elsewhere had resulted in some of the grimmest urban environments. Critics claimed that not only were the changes sought more far-reaching and destructive than necessary but they were being devised against the wishes of the community that would be affected as well as widespread opinion elsewhere. Symbolic of the turnabout in Covent Garden was the decision of Lady Dartmouth in July 1972 to resign from the Chairmanship of the Covent Garden

76
Central Avenue before the market moved out.

Committee: 'No individuals or bodies who represent the general public have supported us, and I have felt increasingly that our proposals are out of tune with public opinion which fears that the area will become a faceless, concrete jungle.'[33]

The decision of the Secretary of State for the Environment following the Public Inquiry was announced in January 1973. While endorsing the proposal for a Comprehensive Development Area it rejected many aspects of the plan, notably the intended road network, calling instead for a new plan to be prepared with 'full public participation'. Supporting the emphasis that had been given to conservation it suggested that such measures could be taken much further, and as if to make the point (while at the same time frustrating large-scale development) it was announced simultaneously that 245 more buildings in the area had been added to the statutory lists.

The intention of the first Draft Plan had been that redevelopment in Covent Garden might start in 1971, ahead of the departure of the market. As it was, when the time for the market's departure finally drew near in 1974 no signs were to be seen of the fundamental changes once promised. Instead a set of discussion papers on the replanning of the area had been issued and the first election held for a local Forum to help in making future policy. Both signalled the beginnings of a return to the practice of gradual, piecemeal renewal such as that followed so astutely by the Bedfords.

Of the events since the market moved out, this work has chosen to concentrate on the most spectacular of all, the restoration of Fowler's building and its reopening as the centrepiece of the area. That is not meant to imply that all else has stood still while the restoration went on, nor that now that work is completed there will be no more changes. Anyone visiting the market is bound to see evidence of much else that has been happening, whether it be simple alterations to existing buildings or quite dramatic developments such as the additions to the Opera House and the completion of new housing in Long Acre and Endell Street. Equally, anyone with half an eye on the newspapers will appreciate that the debate over the area did not cease with the defeat of the 1968 Plan, or with the departure of the market, but carries on with considerable vigour. The subject of the market restoration will no doubt be thrown into the argument—Should it have been done? Has it been done well? Has the building been put to the right use?—but it is at least an episode which being finished can be properly told. By contrast, looking around and beyond the Piazza, other events affecting the area are still far from their conclusion and so are difficult to sum up. In due time perhaps another history will recount their progress and assess their significance.

Appendix

The Restoration Project

Client
The GLC Covent Garden Committee

Architects
Architect to the Council   F B Pooley, CBE
Surveyor of Historic Buildings   B Ashley Barker, OBE
Works Section, Historic Buildings Division   N Harrison, MBE
(Head of Section), T G Bidwell, D J Fowler, J Adams,
J Clenshaw, I McCaig, P Watts, R Wyatt.

Covent Garden Team   G R Holland (Team Leader),
T R Wacher (Deputy Team Leader), A Flint (Surveyor),
Mrs S Marder (Principal Legal Officer).

Director of Mechanical and Electrical Engineering   P C Hoare.
Mechanical Engineering   M J Prince, P A Moulder, K Smith,
P H Jay.
Electrical Engineering   P Bratt, E E Whiston, D Hammond,
P J Dommett.
Structural Engineering   J F Levy, D J Watkins, G Allen,
R G Smith.
Quantity Surveyors   H S Page, A G Page, D A Bray, R Jones,
G Guiness, J Merrifield, T James.
Clerks of Works   T I W Shakelton, R Bonfanti, J Scannell.

Contractors – Stage One
Main Contractor   Walter Lawrence and Son Ltd.
Sub-contractors   Access Scaffolding Ltd (scaffolding), Clean
Walls Ltd (stone cleaning), Demolition Management
Services Ltd (demolitions), Stone Firms Ltd (stone
restoration).

Contractors – Stage Two
Main Contractor   W J Simms, Son and Cooke (Southern) Ltd.
Sub-contractors   Chelsea Glassworks Ltd (glazing), Clean
Walls Ltd (grit blasting), S P Lynch Ltd (painting), E J
Margrie (glazing bars), Metal Stitching Co (cast iron repairs).

Contractors – Stage Three
Main Contractors   F G Minter Ltd (July–August 1977),
Myton Ltd (September 1977–Spring 1980).
Sub-contractors   Acme Gate and Shutter Co (collapsible
steel gates), Annstar Group Ltd (ironmongery), Arvin & Son
Ltd (cork floor tiling), Asphaltic London Ltd (asphalt),
J R Beadon Ltd (French polishing), Bradford's Studio
(signwriting and carving), Bucks Joinery Ltd (joinery supply),
City of Westminster Council (sewage connections), Clark
Hunt & Co Ltd (metalwork), Clean Walls Ltd (grit blasting),
T A Convoy (Mastics) Ltd (mastic pointing), Croft Bros
(London) Ltd (ceramic wall tiling), Curtis Contracts (window
opening gear), David Hobdell Building Ltd (painting and
decorating), Dreadnought Shutter & Door Co Ltd (fire
doors), General Pest Control Ltd (flea eradication), George

Amos & Sons (hot caustic dipping and grit blasting), Gilbert
and Turnball Ltd (stonework, paving and plastic stonework),
The Great Metropolitan Flooring Co Ltd (sanding floors),
Holliday Hall & Co Ltd (electrical installation), Ian Flockton
Developments Ltd (grp gutters), John Healey London Ltd
(smoke vents), Jonathan James Ltd (plastering), Joseph
Jackson and Son Co Ltd (structural steelwork), Leay Glazing
Services Ltd (glazing), Leonards Plumbing Contractors
(lead roofing), Lewis Products Ltd (joinery supply and
repairs), London Electricity Board, London Stone Ltd (grit
blasting), Massrealm Ltd (lights), Matthew Hall Mechanical
Services Ltd (sprinkler installation and mechanical services),
Metal Stitching Co (metalwork repairs), Morceau Fire
Protection Ltd (intumescent mastic), North Thames Gas
Board, Palmers Scaffolding Ltd (scaffolding), Phillips and
Lewis Victoria Ltd (chimney sweeping), Protim Services Ltd
(timber preservation), Robert Adlards and Co Ltd (slate
roofing), Roskel Contracts (London) Ltd (suspended
ceilings), Sealants Techniques Ltd (mastic pointing), Shutter
Contractors Ltd (metal shutters and doors), Sloane and
Davidson (cast iron lamp brackets), Specialist Services Ltd
(diamond cutting), Structural Fireproofers Ltd (mandoseal
fire-proofing), Structural Services (plumbing and drainage),
Thames Water Authority, Unilock Tenon International Ltd
(toilet cubicles), D W Winsor Ltd (lanterns).

Notes

Abbreviations

BOL   Bedford Estate papers held at the Bedford Estate Office, 29a, Montague Street, London, WC1.

CG/E   Bedford Estate papers deposited at the Greater London Record Office, County Hall, London, SE1.

CGC   Greater London Council, Covent Garden Committee. The title of this Committee changed as follows: June 1970–March 1973, the Covent Garden Joint Development Committee; May 1973–November 1974, Covent Garden Development Committee; December 1974–   , the Covent Garden Committee.

MGA   Minutes of the Market Gardeners, Nurserymen and Farmers Association.

PP   Parliamentary Papers.

SOL   F H W Sheppard, ed, *Survey of London*, Vol XXXVI, The Parish of St Paul, Covent Garden (1970).

Chapter 1

1   SOL, p 53.

2   The evolution of these building regulations is discussed in Norman G Brett-James, *The Growth of Stuart London* (1935), pp 67–126, and in John Summerson, 'The Surveyorship of Inigo Jones, 1615–43', in H M Colvin ed *The History of the King's Works*, Vol III (1485–1660) Part 1 (1975), pp 140–3.

3   Robert Ashton, *The English Civil War* (1978), p 73.

4   Summerson, op cit, p 143.

5   SOL, p 2.

6   Ibid, pp 3–4, 26–34. Issac de Caus may have also designed the grotto at Woburn, one of the Bedfords' country seats.

7   Quoted in John Summerson, 'Inigo Jones', *Proceedings of the British Academy* Vol L (1964), p 171n.

8   SOL, pp 99–100.

9   M J Power, 'The East and West in Early-Modern London', in E W Ives, R J Knecht and J J Scarisbrick eds, *Wealth and Power in Tudor England* (1978), p 180.

10   Alchin Collection on Markets, Vol 2, pp 119–20 (Corporation of London Record Office).

11   Details of all the existing and proposed markets in seventeenth century London are given in Patrick V McGrath, 'The Marketing of Food, Fodder and Livestock in the London area in the Seventeenth Century' (unpublished University of London M A thesis, 1948), pp 243–347.

12   Repertories of the Court of Aldermen, 30th October 1649 (Corporation of London Record Office).

13   SOL, p 130.

14   Patrick V McGrath, op cit, p 74.

15   SOL, pp 131–3.

16   M Dorothy George, *London Life in the Eighteenth Century* (1925), pp 83–4, 347.

17   *A Brief Description of the Cities of London and Westminster* (1770), p XXVIII.

18   SOL, p 133.

19   CG/E/9/16/1–4, *King's Bench Suit, Duke of Bedford v Richard White*, 1819; 9/17/1–4, *King's Bench Suit, Duke of Bedford v Aaron Emmett*, 1819; 9/18/1–4, *King's Bench Suit, Duke of Bedford v John Page*, 1820.

20   *John Bull*, 27th November 1825, p 379; 5th December 1825, p 391.

21   CG/E/10/25, Letter from J H Fisher to W G Adam, 25th December 1826.

22   BOL, Letter from W G Adam to T P Brown, 18th September 1826. After the sixth Duke's death in 1839 his successor commented on how 'both the Adams continued, for more than thirty years, to remonstrate with my father (and in pretty strong terms too) on his annual excess of expenditure over income and his consequent increasing debt. It is very creditable to them' (*Letters to Lord G William Russell from Various Writers 1817–1845*, 1915, p 357).

23   BOL, Annual Report 1827.

24   *Journals of the House of Commons*, Vol LXXXIII, pp 258, 482.

25   Fowler's career is dealt with in two articles by Jeremy Taylor, in *Architectural Review*, Vol CXXXV (March 1964), pp 174–82 and *Architectural History*, Vol XI (1968), pp 57–74.

26   Charles Fowler, *Description of the Plan for the Revival of Hungerford Market* (1829); J Robinson, 'A Descriptive Account . . . of Hungerford New Market', *Architectural Magazine*, Vol I (1834), pp 53–62.

27   T L Donaldson, 'Memoir of the Late Charles Fowler', *RIBA Proceeding 1867–8*, p 7.

28   'It is of too general a character, and attempts too much in trying to unite Leadenhall, Billingsgate, and Covent Garden Markets' (Peter Cunningham, *Hand-Book of London*, 2nd ed 1850, p 240).

29   CG/E/10/23, Letter from W G Adam to J H Fisher, 11th October 1827.

30   BOL, Letter from W G Adam to Christopher Haedy,

4th January 1828; *The Gardener's Magazine*, Vol VII (1831), p 265.

31 CG/E/10/25, *A Short Description of the Model of Covent Garden Market*. There are two versions of this document, one dated December 1826 and one undated. They are identical in most respects except that the former suggests the erection of a monument to Shakespeare at the east end of the market.

32 Ibid. Fowler was about to make extensive use of cast iron in the roof and dome of the conservatory he designed for Syon House.

33 CG/E/10/25, Letter from Charles Fowler to W G Adam, 31st December 1827; BOL, Letters from W G Adam to Christopher Haedy, 2nd and 4th January 1828.

34 CG/E/10/25, Notes from the Duke of Bedford, 3rd and 18th December 1829.

35 *Gardener's Magazine*, op cit, pp 265, 267.

36 The tenders received were:
William Cubitt: £34,850.
Henry Lee and Sons: £36,286.
Samuel Baker and Sons: £37,540.
(CG/E/10/25).

37 BOL, Letter from W G Adam to Christopher Haedy, 20th September 1828; CG/E/10/26, Letter from G Sinclair to the Duke of Bedford, 8th June 1830.

38 When the large iron roof was built over the north court-yard 1888–9 Fowler's roof was moved to a site between Russell Street and the Floral Hall, where it survived until recently. Fowler also designed a freestanding roof, this time of cantilever construction, for the fish market in the lower hall at Hungerford Market (illust in Nicholas Taylor, *Monuments of Commerce*, 1968, pp 28–9).

39 CG/E/10/25, Mr Fowler's statement of additions to works since the tenders were made, 6th December 1828. Tests made at the time of the restoration suggested that the stone may have come from a quarry near Edinburgh (though was that the original stonework or that dating from the Cubitt renovations of 1871?). The best available match for use in the restoration was a sandstone from Hollington in Derbyshire.

40 BOL, Letter from W G Adam to Christopher Haedy, 31st October 1828.

41 Letter written by Charles Fowler in Exeter Markets Records Box 2, File 6 (Devon Record Office).

42 BOL, Receipts and Payments by Mr Haedy, Vol I, pp 167, 171; CG/E/10/27, Letter from Christopher Haedy to Charles Fowler, 8th August 1831 and reply from Fowler, 10th August 1831.

43 *Gardener's Magazine*, op cit, pp 270–1; CG/E/10/26, Letter from Charles Fowler to Christopher Haedy, 26th February 1829.

44 BOL, Receipts and Payments op cit, p 175; Annual Report 1832–3; Royal Commission on Market Rights and Tolls, *PP* 1888 (5550–1), LIII, Q 2572.

45 MGA, Letter from Christopher Haedy, 18th February 1858. The figures quoted by Haedy were:

Cost of rebuilding the market: £70,000
Rent paid before rebuilding: £2,500
Av net receipts from market: £5,899
Therefore sum available to compensate for rebuilding: £3,399

46 CG/E/10/31, Statement of Weekly Rents in Covent Garden Market.

47 Peter Cunningham, op cit, p 144.

48 BOL, Letter from W G Adam to Christopher Haedy, 14th October 1828.

Chapter 2

1 *The Gardener's Magazine*, Vol VII (1831), pp 275–7. There was an earlier, briefer description of the building in ibid, Vol VI (1830), pp 513–4. Other reports confined themselves more closely to praising the superior accommodation it offered, eg *The British Farmer's Magazine*: 'The facility of approach, security of stowage, and commodiousness for exhibition, is all highly creditable to the architect' (Vol IV, August 1830, p 368).

2 Walter M Stern, 'The Baroness' Market: The History of a Noble Failure', *Guildhall Miscellany*, Vol XI (September 1966), pp 353–66.

3 *The Architectural Magazine*, Vol II (March 1835), pp 129–33; K Grady, 'The Provision Markets in Leeds 1822–29', *Thoresby Miscellany*, Vol 16, Part 3 (1976), pp 168, 174; *The Birmingham Market Hall* (Birmingham, 1935), pp 5–11; Jeremy Taylor, 'Charles Fowler: Master of Markets', *Architectural Review*, Vol CXXXV (March 1964), pp 180–1. Of the markets mentioned only the Higher Market at Exeter survives, and its integration into a new shopping precinct has been rather crudely achieved.

4 14th May 1858, p 493. A writer in the *Food Journal* expressed the same opinion more forcibly: 'It is impossible for the thoughtful saunterer to avoid the conviction, which is forced upon him at every turn, that the market is far from what it ought to be. Mr Fowler's plans appear to have ignored its purposes, and certainly its probable development' (Vol 1, June 1st 1870, pp 269–70).

5 George Augustus Sala, 'Under the Piazzas', *Temple Bar*, Vol IX (August 1863), p 99.

6 (W H Leeds), 'Architecture of Shop Fronts', *Westminster Review*, Vol XXXVI (October 1841), p 452; see also the *Builder*, 27th February 1858, pp 145–6.

7 *Building News*, 14th May 1858, p 493.

8 *Civil Engineer and Architect's Journal*, 1st April 1866, pp 108–10; *Nottinghamshire Guardian*, 1st June 1866, p 3; Benjamin Poole, *Coventry: Its History and Antiquities* (1870), pp 330–2. Coventry Market was destroyed in the Second World War: Derby Market Hall still stands but with major alterations made in 1938 and 1965.

9 CG/E/10/29, Petition from Tenants of Stands in the Long Market, March 1831.

10 BOL, Annual Report 1840, p 48; Metropolitan Buildings Office, Cases of Special Supervision, Vol 22, pp 10–16 (Greater London Record Office).

11 BOL, Annual Report 1860, p 8; MGA, Minutes of Meetings 16th August, 13th and 15th November 1860.

12 BOL, Annual Report 1871, Vol 2, pp 4–5.

13 *Building News*, 28th July 1871, p 68.

14 MGA, Minutes of Meeting 13th March 1852 (copy of statement sent to the Duke of Bedford).

15 *The Times,* 7th September 1871, p 5; BOL, London Reports, Vol 1, pp 217–8; CG/E/10/48, Petitions and Memoranda for and against Roofing Parts of the Market, 1862–73.

16 BOL, London Reports, Vol 1, pp 274–6; there are various roof designs in CG/E/5/3/16–7 and 5/3/35.

17 *Builder,* 17th October 1874, p 863; *Building News*, 27th August 1875, p 217.

18 MGA, Minutes of Meetings 6th March and 3rd October 1876; BOL, Annual Reports 1889, pp 169–70.

19 BOL, London Reports, Vol 3, pp 255, 293; *Covent Garden Gazette and Market Record* Vol II (6th March 1886), p 116.

20 *Builder,* 15th December 1855, pp 603–4. Gye's scheme predated by at least ten years Sir Joseph Paxton's proposal for an iron and glass arcade to encircle London, called the Great Victorian Way (George F Chadwick, *The Works of Sir Joseph Paxton*, 1961, pp 208–13).

21 *Illustrated London News*, 5th September 1857, p 246; F H W Sheppard, ed *The Survey of London*, Vol XXXV (1970), pp 81–2.

22 CG/E/8/10/18, Resumé of Correspondence between Bedford Office and Frederick Gye *c*1855–60, pp 10–11, 60.

23 *Builder,* 2nd April 1859, pp 235–6; *Building News*, 9th March 1860, p 182, 27th August 1875, p 288. The ironwork of the Floral Hall was supplied by Henry Grissell of the Regent's Canal Ironworks in Hoxston, and the decoration was carried out by Mr Antonio Perrocchi of Cranbourn Street.

24 CG/E/8/10/17, *Notes by Mr Gye as to the Use of the Floral Hall.*

25 Sala, op cit, p 100; BOL, Annual Report 1887, p 174.

26 BOL, Annual Report 1872, Vol 2, pp 17–21; *Building News*, 13th September 1872, p 207.

27 *Journal of Horticulture*, 14th August 1884, p 149; BOL, London Reports, Vol 3, pp 326–7. According to a report made in 1887 the 1871–2 part of the Flower Market cost £15,679 and the 1884–6 part £28,036; in 1886 the net income from rents and tolls in the building was £4,636 (BOL, London Reports, Vol 2, p 77).

28 BOL, Annual Reports 1894, p 193; *Builder,* 1st October 1904, p 340.

29 *Builder,* 5th August 1871, p 604.

30 Royal Commission on Market Rights and Tolls, *PP* 1888 (5550–1), LI II, Q2651.

31 BOL, Annual Report 1891, p 106.

32 Royal Commission, op cit, QQ 2731–2, 4258, 4328–9.

33 Royal Commission on Labour, *PP* 1893–4 (6894–IX), XXXIV, QQ 31,908–65; Charles Booth, *Life and Labour of the People in London*, Second Series, Vol 3 (1903), pp 224–6.

34 Royal Commission on Market Rights and Tolls, *PP* 1890–1 (6268–VI), XXXIX, p 28; BOL, Annual Reports 1881. Vol 2, p 3; 1889, pp 170, 176.

35 BOL, London Reports, Vol 1, p 319. In 1876, when the deputation from the Market Gardeners Association visited the Duke to thank him for roofing the south courtyard, he remarked 'that ultimately he looked forward to the probable acquisition of the Market by a Metropolitan Municipality who would be able to deal with so large a question in a more comprehensive manner than he himself could undertake to do' (ibid, pp 449–50)

36 *Punch,* 14th August 1880, p 71; 9th October 1880, p 162; BOL, Annual Report 1883, Vol 2, pp 4–14.

37 Royal Commission on Market Rights and Tolls, *PP* 1888 (5550–III), LV, Q. 3569; H Keeble Hawson, *Sheffield, The Growth of a City* 1893–1926 (Sheffield, 1968), pp 1–3.

38 CG/E/12/1, Correspondence Relating to the Sale to H Mallaby-Deeley, 1913–14; SOL, pp 50–1.

39 Ministry of Food, Departmental Committee on the Wholesale Food Markets of London, Minutes of Meeting January 31st 1920, p 18; SOL, p 144.

40 SOL, p 147. On the new building at Nine Elms, see *Building,* 14th February 1975, pp 71–86.

Chapter 3

1 On the preservation and loss of London buildings see Hermione Hobhouse, *Lost London* (1971) and Greater London Council, *Historic Buildings in London* (1975). The Euston Portico case is described in detail in *Architectural Review*, Vol CXXXI (April 1962), pp 234–8.

2 G G Scott, *A Plea for the Faithful Restoration of our Ancient Churches* (1850), p 29. The International Charter for the Conservation and Restoration of Monuments and Sites (Venice, 1964) puts great emphasis on the retention of the later additions made to a building (and by implication the retention of important buildings within an older layout): 'The valid contributions of all periods to the building of a monument must be respected, since unity of style is not the aim of restoration. When a building includes the superimposed work of different periods, the revealing of the underlying state can only be justified in exceptional circumstances and when what is removed is of little interest and the material which is brought to light is of great historical, archaeological or aesthetic value, and its state of preservation good enough to justify the action' (Article 11).

3 London County Council, *Covent Garden Area – Redevelopment* (Report TP 542, 20th November 1964), pp 1, 4. The same report listed 'the old market buildings in Covent Garden' as 'worthy of preservation in any forseeable circumstances' (Appendix C).

4 Greater London Council, *Covent Garden's Moving* (1968), pp 52, 64; Fig 13.

5 *Covent Garden's Moving*, p 46; GLC Historic Buildings Board, Resolution 17th February 1970.

6 CGC, Report CG138; Resolution, 5th December 1973; *Times*, 19th November 1973, p 4.

7 CGC, Report CG60; Resolution, 21st June 1972. The Architectural Association put forward a more developed proposal in 1974 in which they were to use part of the building while the rest was taken up by commercial or community uses (*Architects' Journal*, 24th April 1974, pp 892–3).

8 CGC, Resolution 5th December 1973; GLC Minutes, 23rd July 1974, p 393. The GLC paid the Market Authority £6 million for their properties. The main market building cost £388,000 which was its open market value taking into account its being listed.

9 2 & 3 George VI, *c*XCVII, sec 149 (g). The same Act mentions the exemption of other markets including the Caledonian Market, Billingsgate, and Spitalfields; also railway stations and dock buildings.

10 *Times*, 21st December 1949, p 4; 22nd December, p 4.

11 CGC, Reports CG236 and CG247; Resolution, 4th December 1974.

12 CGC, Report CG202; Resolution, 11th September 1974.

13 All the contracts were of a fixed price with fluctuations, variation orders being drawn up for every change made during the progress of the work. Such was the complexity of the project that it has been argued that contracting by schedule of rates – measuring and pricing the work once completed – might have been more satisfactory. That method would though have had the disadvantage of producing less initial information on which Council committees could base their decisions, as well as less financial control over the project.

14 CGC, Resolution 19th June 1974; Report CG606.

15 CGC, Reports CG343 and CG606; Resolution, 3rd December 1975. W J Simms Son and Cooke (Southern) Ltd went bankrupt at the very end of their contract.

16 CGC, Report CG606; Resolutions, 22nd September 1975 and 10th November 1975.

17 CGC, Report CG717; Resolution, 16th March 1977; *Contract Journal*, 11th August 1977, p 2.

18 CGC, Chairman's Decision, 26th August 1977.

19 Cleaning revealed that the north-west pavilion, which was severely damaged by bombing in the war, had been rebuilt with its upper storey rendered to simulate Portland Stone. There has been no attempt in the restoration to set this anomaly right.

20 The only thing plastic stonework does not contain is plastic. It is generally made up of stone dust, sand, white cement and colouring.

21 The standards required to meet the fire regulations in cases such as these are laid down in the London Building (Construction) By-Laws (1972), Tables F and G.

22 Designs for a lighting scheme using gas were made but electricity was finally selected because of the high mainten- ence costs of gas lighting. The electric fittings in the shop units have been supplied by the tenants.

Chapter 4

1 There are of course plenty of examples of commercial and civic buildings whose restoration has not involved any change of use, for instance the admirable rehabilitation of the mid-Victorian Covered Market at Darlington, County Durham, carried out 1978–9.

2 Nina Gruen, 'Gestalt Magnetism or What is Special about Speciality Shopping Centers?', *Urban Land*, Vol XXXVII (January 1978), pp 3–9; Keith Scott and Ronald Gammie, 'Speciality Centres', *Estates Gazette*, 28th July 1979, pp 353–5. Although the most well-known speciality centres make use of old buildings there are a number which have been purpose-built.

3 Michael Lee and Elizabeth Kent, 'Brent Cross Study', *Donaldsons Research Report* 4 (1977), p 3.

4 Greater London Council, *Covent Garden's Moving* (1968), p 52; *Covent Garden. The Next Step* (1971), p 11.

5 CGC, Report GC58.

6 CGC, Report CG178.

7 CGC, Reports CG268 and CG289; Resolution, 26th February 1975. Later, as the third contract neared completion, it was decided that some of the first floor spaces might be used for retailing.

8 CGC, Reports CG786 and CG812; Resolution, 14th February 1978.

9 CGC, Reports CG863 and CG877.

10 Courage's, the pub tenants, have been allowed to extend their premises by flooring over the west end of Central Avenue.

11 CGC, Report CG853. The policy of allowing craftsmen and others to use the pushcarts beneath the canopies at Faneuil Hall Marketplace has been a great success.

12 The idea of locating a conference centre in Covent Garden was dropped in July 1973 (GLC Minutes, 3rd July 1973, pp 327–9).

13 CGC, Reports CG512, CG520, CG589 and CG680. It had been decided earlier that the basement of the Flower Market and the 1904–5 addition at the corner of Wellington Street and Russell Street should become a theatre museum largely made up of material from the theatre collection at the Victoria and Albert Museum. At the time of writing this project had not been started.

14 The damage to the ironwork in the Flower Market may have been the result of a Zeppelin bombing raid during the First World War.

15 A E Brown, *Faneuil Hall and Faneuil Hall Market* (Boston, Mass, 1900), pp 171–88.

16 *Faneuil Hall Markets Boston, Massachusetts. Historical Study* (Boston, Mass, Architectural Heritage Inc and the Society for New England Antiquities, 1968), pp 47–8. Alexander

Parris also showed his ingenuity in the design of the dome that surmounts the centre of the Quincy Market, which was in fact two domes the one suspended from the other, and in his use of iron columns under compression in the ground floor arcade of the same building.

17 For instance, the account in *Architectural Record*, Vol CLXII (December 1977), pp 122, 126–7.

18 *Boston Sunday Globe*, 29th October 1972.

19 Comments made by Benjamin Thompson and Jane McC Thompson at the time of the reopening of the Quincy Market building in August 1976, reprinted in *Architectural Record*, op cit, p 124.

20 There had been existing canopies but these were removed at an earlier stage in the restoration.

21 *Boston Sunday Globe*, 2nd September 1979.

Chapter 5

1 Donald J Olsen, *The Growth of Victorian London* (1976), pp 127–8.

2 Select Committee of the House of Commons on Town Holdings, *PP* 1887 (260), XIII, Q 11398.

3 Ibid, Q 11249.

4 SOL, pp 230, 233–5.

5 Ibid, pp 151–2, 156–7, 166–9.

6 Ibid, p 81.

7 Olsen, op cit, p 127.

8 *Builder*, 24th August 1878, p 875; BOL, London Reports, Vol 1, p 277.

9 Anthony S Wohl, *The Eternal Slum, Housing and Social Policy in Victorian London* (1977), pp 26–35.

10 SOL, pp 226–9, 186–7.

11 Seventh Report of the Commissioners . . . (for) Improving the Metropolis, *PP* 1851 (1356), XXIX, p 5; SOL, pp 43–4.

12 *Illustrated London News*, 9th June 1860, pp 566, 568; *Builder*, 10th December 1864, pp 901–2; *Building News*, 17th June 1864, p 464.

13 G A Sala, *Twice Round the Clock* (1859), pp 164–5; Select Committee on Artizans' and Labourers' Dwellings Improvement, *PP* 1881 (358), VII, QQ 1923, 1931; London County Council, *The Housing Question in London 1855–1900* (1901), pp 126–30.

14 *The Housing Question*, op cit, pp 130–2.

15 BOL, London Reports, Vol 2, pp 7–11.

16 Drury Lane Christian Mission, '*A Light that Shineth in a Dark Place*' (1874); Cicely Hamilton and Lilian Baylis *The Old Vic* (1928), pp 276–8.

17 SOL, p 48; LCC, *Opening of Kingsway and Aldwych by His Majesty the King, 18th October 1905*.

18 BOL, Annual Report 1861, p 117; 1862, pp 75–6.

19 *John Tallis's London Street Views* 1838–1840 (new ed 1969) pp 194–5; *Builder*, 8th November 1873, p 896; *Post Office Directories*.

20 A L Humphreys, 'Long Acre and the Coachbuilders', *Notes and Queries* 18th October 1941, pp 212–15; 25th October 1941, pp 228–30; *Post Office Directories*.

21 *George Monro Ltd 1862–1935. Over Seventy Years of Fruit Distribution* (1935).

22 *The Fruit-Grower*, 3rd March 1938, pp 355–8.

23 Ministry of Food, Fourth Report of the Departmental Committee on the Wholesale Food Markets of London, *PP* 1921 (1341), XII, p 7; The Fantus Company, *Study for the Re-Location of Covent Garden Market London* (1963), p 27.

24 *London Replanned. The Royal Academy Planning Committee's Interim Report* (1942), pp 10–11. Both this plan, and the Forshaw-Abercrombie County Of London Plan of 1943, recommended that Covent Garden and other London markets should be moved to near the edge of the London area.

25 London County Council, *Covent Garden Area-Redevelopment* (Report TP 542, 20th November 1964), p 43.

26 Greater London Council, *Covent Garden's Moving* (1968), p 32.

27 *Covent Garden's Moving*, op cit, pp 19–20, 36.

28 Ibid, pp 22–3, 36.

29 Ibid, pp 20–2, 57–8, 103–6. In 1972 the route of the main west-east 'line of character' running through the area was declared a Conservation Area.

30 Ibid, pp 37–9, 55–61. It was suggested as an alternative that the Strand relief road might carry two-way traffic allowing the Strand to become a pedestrian street. This alternative was discounted in the Revised Plan.

31 Greater London Council, *Covent Garden. The Next Step* (1971), pp 26–7.

32 Colin Amery et al, 'Save the Garden', *Architectural Review*, Vol CL II (July 1972), p 20.

33 *Times*, 29th July 1972, p 1.

Bibliography

Manuscript Material

Bedford Estate Records
The records relating to Covent Garden Market have been deposited by the Trustees of the Bedford Estate in the Greater London Record Office, County Hall, SE1. These include correspondence and papers relating to the construction of Fowler's market building 1826–30, architectural drawings and records of the market's administration; also correspondence between Frederick Gye and the Bedford Office concerning the construction and management of the Floral Hall.

Other records relating to the general administration of the Bedford Estate, many of which include reference to the market, are held at the Bedford Estate Office, 29a Montague Street, London WC1. These include the Annual Reports 1827–8, 1831–98 and the London Reports 1869–1924, plus the correspondence of the Dukes of Bedford with their agents and stewards.

The Market Gardeners, Nurserymen and Farmers Association
Four volumes of the minutes of this association, covering the years 1841–52, 1875–1920 are held at the National Farmers' Union, Agriculture House, Knightsbridge, London, SW1. One further volume, covering the years 1851–65, is held by T J Poupart Ltd, New Covent Garden Market, London, SW8.

William Cubitt and Company
Two volumes of estmates, 1883–1912, which include many references to repairs and alterations carried out by Cubitts at the market, are held by Holland, Hannen and Cubitts Ltd, Cubitt House, Madeira Walk, Windsor, Berks.

Charles Booth manuscripts
The manuscript notebooks used in the preparation of Charles Booth's *Life and Labour of the People in London* are in the collection of the London School of Economics. The volumes covering the subject of the market are Group A Vols 22–3, and Group B Vol 133.

Greater London Council Records

Copies of the reports presented to the Covent Garden Committee and the Historic Buildings Committee (the two Council committees most closely concerned with the restoration of the market building) are kept in the Greater London Record Office at County Hall. The day by day files, architectural drawings and other documents relating to the project are still in the hands of the Covent Garden Team, 1–4 King Street, London, WC2 and the Historic Buildings Division, County Hall.

The main published planning documents on the area are:
Covent Garden's Moving. The Covent Garden Area Draft Plan (1968).

Covent Garden. The Next Step. The Revised Plan for the Proposed Comprehensive Development Area (1971).
Covent Garden Area. Local Plan. Discussion Papers and Reports of Survey, 6 Vols (1974).
Covent Garden Action Area Plan (1978).

Government Publications

Seventh Report of the Commissioners . . . (for) Improving the Metropolis, *PP* 1851 (1356) XXIX.
Select Committee of the House of Commons on Artizans' and Labourers' Dwellings Improvement, *PP* 1881 (358) VII.
Return for each Municipal Borough as to whom the Market Rights belong, how acquired, receipts for 1885 etc, *PP* 1886 (221) LVI.
Select Committee of the House of Commons on Town Holdings, *PP* 1887 (260) XIII.
Royal Commission on Market Rights and Tolls, *PP* 1888 (5550–I) LII; 1890–1 (6268–VI) XXXIX.
Royal Commission on Labour, *PP* 1893–4 (6894–IX) XXXIV.
Ministry of Food, First Report of the Departmental Committee on the Wholesale Food Markets of London, *PP* 1920 (634) XVII.
Ministry of Food, Fourth Report of the Departmental Committee on the Wholesale Food Markets of London, *PP* 1921 (1341) XII.
Ministry of Food, Departmental Committee on the Wholesale Food Markets of London 1919–21, Minutes of proceedings (British Library pressmark BS13/1).
Ministry of Agriculture and Fisheries, Departmental Committee on the Distribution and Prices of Agricultural Produce: Interim Report on Fruit and Vegetables, *PP* 1923 (1892) IX.
Ministry of Agriculture and Fisheries, *Economic Series No 26: Markets and Fairs in England and Wales* (1930).
Report of the Committee on Horticultural Marketing, *PP* 1956–7 (61) XIV.
Select Committee of the House of Commons on the Covent Garden Market Bill, *PP* 1960–1 (140) IV.

Books, Articles etc

This list does not include detailed references to articles in journals such as the *Builder*, *Building News*, and the *Architect*. The place of publication for books in London unless otherwise stated.

Published Before 1939
Edward A Arnold, 'The London Flower Trade', *Nineteenth Century*, Vol XVIII (August 1885), pp 328–37.
Charles Booth, *Life and Labour of the People in London*, 1st ser Vol 1 (1902), pp 192–204; 2nd ser Vol 3 (1903), pp 214–29.
Norman G Brett-James, *The Growth of Stuart London* (1935).
E Beresford Chancellor, *The Annals of Covent Garden and its Neighbourhood* (1930).

Copy of a Letter Addressed to Dawson Turner Esq on the Occasion of the Death of the Late Duke of Bedford (Glasgow, 1840).

George Dodd, *The Food of London* (1856).

T L Donaldson, 'Memoir of the Late Charles Fowler, Fellow' *RIBA Proceedings* 1867–8, pp 1–15.

H Evershed, 'Market-Gardening', *Journal of the Royal Agricultural Society of England*, 2nd ser Vol VII (1871), pp 420–36.

Charles Fowler, *Description of the Plan for the Revival of Hungerford Market* (1829).

Gardener's Magazine, Vol VI (1830), pp 105,513–4; Vol VII (1831), pp 267–77.

W W Glenny, 'The Fruit and Vegetable Markets of the Metropolis', *Journal of the Royal Agricultural Society of England*, 3rd ser Vol VII (1896), pp 53–67.

London County Council, *London Markets. Special Report of the Public Control Committee* (1893).

C Maughan, *Markets of London* (1931).

Henry Mayhew, *London Labour and the London Poor*, Vol 1 (1851).

Morning Chronicle, December 5th 1850, pp 5–6.

The New Survey of London Life and Labour, Vol V (1933).

James Newlands, *A Short Description of the Markets and Market System of Paris, with Notes on the Markets of London* (Liverpool, 1865).

W J Passingham, *London's Markets. Their Origin and History* (1935).

J M Philp, 'Covent Garden Market', *Food Journal*, Vol I (June 1st 1870), pp 267–71.

Report of the Late Important Trial in the Court of Common Pleas in which John Lowden and Robert Prince . . . were Plaintiffs and John Hierons, a Market Gardener, The Defendent (1817).

Report of the Proceedings in Parliament Upon the Late Opposition to the Bill for the Regulation of Covent Garden Market (1813).

George Augustus Sala, 'Under the Piazzas', *Temple Bar*, IX (August 1863), pp 98–107.

William Senior, 'Covent Garden Market', *Good Words*, Vol XXXII (1891), pp 20–27.

C W Shaw, *The London Market Gardens* (1879).

J Thomson and Adolphe Smith, *Street Life in London* (1877).

(Sidney Webb), *The Scandal of London's Markets*, Fabian Tract No 36, nd (1891).

Westminster City Council, *Covent Garden Market: a Report by the Town Clerk* (1926).

(Andrew Wynter), 'The London Commissariat', *Quarterly Review* Vol CXC (September 1854), pp 271–308.

Published Since 1939

Colin Amery et al, 'Save the Garden', *Architectural Review*, Vol CLII (July 1972), pp 16–32.

Mary Cathcart Borer, *Covent Garden* (1967).

Clive Boursnell, *Covent Garden Market* (1977).

Kathryn L Buzzacott, 'London's Markets: Their Growth, Characteristics and Functions', unpublished University of London PhD thesis, 1972.

David Cannadine, 'Aristocratic Indebtedness in the Nineteenth Century: the Case Reopened', *Economic History Review*, 2nd ser Vol XXX (1977), pp 624–50.

David Cannadine, 'From Feudal Lords to Figureheads', *Urban History Yearbook* (1978), pp 23–35.

Peter Chapman, 'Changing Objectives at Covent Garden?', *Official Architecture and Planning*, Vol XXXIV (April 1971), pp 311–2.

Terry Christensen, *Neighbourhood Survival* (Chalmington, Dorset, 1979).

Ian Christie, 'Covent Garden, Approaches to Urban Renewal', *Town Planning Review*, Vol XLV (January 1974), pp 30–62.

'Covent Garden Area Draft Plan', *Town and Country Planning*, Vol XXXVII (April 1969), pp 176–84.

'Covent Garden Carve Up', *Architectural Design*, Vol XLI (July 1971), pp 402–11.

Covent Garden Market Authority, *Annual Reports*, 1961–2 onwards.

The Fantus Company, *Study for the Re-location of Covent Garden Market, London* (1963).

P V McGrath, 'The Marketing of Food, Fodder and Livestock in the London Area in the Seventeenth Century', unpublished University of London MA thesis, 1948.

Tony McIntyre, 'Covent Garden: Grand Planning to Muddling Along', *Architectural Design*, Vol XLVI (March 1976), pp 144–48.

Jim Monahan, 'Up Against the Planners in Covent Garden', in Peter Hain ed, *Community Politics* (1976).

Donald J Olsen, *Town Planning in London. The Eighteenth and Nineteenth Centuries* (1964).

Donald J Olsen, *The Growth of Victorian London* (1976).

Simon Pembroke, *Covent Garden. Summary of Objections Made Local Public Inquiry . . . 6th July–16th September* 1971 (1972).

Nikolaus Pevsner, *A History of Building Types* (1976).

F H W Sheppard, ed, *Survey of London* Vol XXXVI, the Parish of St Paul Covent Garden (1970).

David Spring, *The English Landed Estate in the Nineteenth Century: its Administration* (Baltimore, Maryland, 1963).

John Summerson, 'Inigo Jones', *Proceedings of the British Academy*, Vol L (1964), pp 169–92.

John Summerson, *Inigo Jones* (Harmondsworth, Middx, 1964).

Jeremy Taylor, 'Charles Fowler; Master of Markets', *Architectural Review*, Vol CXXXV (March 1964), pp 174–82.

Jeremy Taylor, 'Charles Fowler (1792–1867): A Centenary Memoir', *Architectural History*, Vol XI (1968), pp 57–74.

F M L Thompson, *English Landed Society in the Nineteenth Century* (1963).

Ronald Webber, *Covent Garden, Mud-Salad Market* (1969).

Index